Muhammad ALI

His Fights in the Ring

ROBERT WALKER

MIDAS BOOKS

By the same author
Rachmaninoff — his life and times

First published 1978 by
Midas Books
12 Dene Way, Speldhurst,
Tunbridge Wells, Kent TN3 0NX

Walker, Robert
  Muhammad Ali, his fights in the ring.
  1. Muhammad Ali
  I. Title
  796.8'3'0924   GV1132.M84

ISBN 0-85936-161-6

Filmset in Plantin by The Humble Wordsmith, Tonbridge, Kent.
Printed in Great Britain by offset lithography by
Billing & Sons Ltd, Guildford, London and Worcester

Contents

                    *   *   *   *

Foreword

The main body of this book — the descriptions and analyses of the fights of Muhammad Ali — has been written from notes which I compiled over sixteen years, since I saw the Cassius Clay-Archie Moore fight in 1962.

In writing this book, I have naturally had recourse to material other than the accounts of the fights I made at the time, and I would like to acknowledge the debt I owe, and to suggest for further reading, a number of previous books on Muhammad Ali.

This book is mainly concerned with Ali's boxing, but for the other aspects of his life which are mentioned herein, the following books have been invaluable:

... *Sting Like a Bee* by José Torres 1971
> Abelard-Schumann Ltd/Coronet Books

Loser and Still Champion by Budd Schulberg 1972
> Doubleday and Company/New English Library

The Holy Warrior — Muhammad Ali by Don Atyeo and Felix Dennis 1975
> Bunch Books/H. Bunch Associates Ltd

The Greatest — My Own Story by Muhammad Ali with Richard Durham 1975
> Hart-Davis, MacGibbon Ltd/Mayflower Books Ltd

Torres's book is one of the greatest of all boxing books: a world champion boxer himself, he writes with the unparalleled insight that can only come from having done the job personally. Budd Schulberg's book is more philosophical, as one would expect from such a distinguished author. Don Atyeo and Felix Dennis have done a first-class job. Their book contains much detail of Ali's life, together with a great many pictures, and ends with a lengthy account of Ali regaining the championship from George Foreman in 1974. Ali's own book is also, obviously, indispensable, but it is not a straightforward autobiography, tending to digress into other subjects (religion, politics, marriage), leaving large parts of his life unrecorded.

On re-reading the accounts I wrote at the time I saw the fights (either live or on film) I have had occasion to change one or two things in the light of later developments. But, generally speaking, I have kept the original style of each fight, in the belief that a contemporary account, made while the event is fresh in the mind, has a validity which overrides any stylistic lapses. I have persisted — no doubt inadvisedly — in my own impressions and opinions, even though, from checking other accounts, I would seem to be in the minority in some cases.

I have to acknowledge the great help extended to me by Bob Mee of *Boxing News*, in checking and verifying many factual points. The Professional Fight Record, which is Appendix B, is based on that published in Ali's autobiography, but extended and corrected. By using this Appendix, in conjunction with the table shown at the heading of each fight, it is possible to get a complete picture of Ali's record. In the case of later fights, Ali's contracts often call for a percentage of peripheral takings (the gate, closed-circuit tv, etc) and these additional amounts are almost impossible to ascertain. Therefore the final column (Ali's purses) should almost certainly be increased. I have not listed money received from exhibitions or other fights, which is again very difficult to obtain and has no place in a Professional Record: in 1975, Ali estimated his exhibition takings at $1,500,000. Knockouts and technical knockouts, including those occasions where the fight ended between rounds, are all shown as 'KOs'.

Generally speaking, I have followed published figures, but occasionally there is a conflict and the facts are difficult to obtain. On such occasions — and mercifully they are rare — I have followed Ali's own account.

I must thank my publisher, Ian Morley-Clarke, for his keen enthusiasm for the project, and Brian Jewell for his invaluable picture research. Finally, with much love, I must thank my wife for her constant encouragement and support while the book was written.

London SE12   R.W.
October 1978

CHAPTER ONE

The Name of the Game

Boxing is a serious, dangerous business. It is often misunderstood. In cold blood, two men, before a paying audience, inflict pain and wounds on each other, running the risk of being killed in the process. For those taking part, it is an unemotional sport, for no boxer who allowed his emotions to get the better of his reason ever won a fight. The object is two-fold: prevent the other man from hitting you, and hit him in the process. It is done at speed. There is a time-limit. There are strict rules, and two unwritten laws.

These laws are simple. The first is: you must move. If you do not move, you will be hit. The second is: you must hit. If you do not hit, you will not overcome your opponent and so prevent him hitting you.

With professional boxers, these laws are instinctive, primeval. What raises boxing above the street-corner brawl is the skill and manner by which these laws are applied. The boxer has to try to be one move ahead, to guess what his opponent is going to do next, and to respond accordingly, at the same time as planning his own attack. In these terms, boxing is an intellectual pursuit, like chess, algebra or fugal composition. As in those disciplines, the subtlety, the dramatic juxtaposition and the inevitability of the best examples raises the fight to a totally different plane.

Just as a motor racing champion cannot win a race with a faulty car, so no boxer can win if his body is not at its peak. Boxing is therefore not only physical. The body is the beginning, but in addition the boxer needs skill, tactical ability, psychological insight, moral fibre, sensitivity and intelligence.

These are fine qualities, and a great champion must contain elements of all of them. With Muhammad Ali we have the man who combines these qualities in a boxer to a degree unparalleled in human experience. Not all who watch boxing are motivated by these ideals, for it is perfectly possible to view the sport at various levels, in the same way as a great painting, a great piece of music, or a great cathedral can make a powerful impact on the observer who might not necessarily appreciate the less obvious qualities which those things possess.

By studying Muhammad Ali's life in the ring, a man who by common consent is the greatest boxer the world has ever seen, we can observe those qualities in action. Boxing is an honourable profession, and its best elements, in the greatest fights of the greatest fighter, remain for all time for those who have the interest and understanding to grasp them.

1

CHAPTER TWO

Outside the Ring

Muhammad Ali (or Cassius Clay as he was then) became a professional boxer in 1960. By 1964 he had fought his way to the top of his profession, through a succession of wins that remained unbroken for 11 years — although $3\frac{1}{2}$ of those years were spent away from the ring in forced exile. No-one can study Muhammad Ali's career for five minutes without becoming aware that his charismatic personality extends far beyond boxing. His activities outside the ring have made him as well-known a character as his exploits inside it. His boxing career is what mainly concerns us in this book, but we cannot dismiss those outside activities entirely : a man is the sum total of all his conduct, and only by placing those elements in their proper place can we fully appreciate the major part of Ali's life — his boxing.

In the first place, there is his mouth. Before Cassius Clay erupted on the scene, many boxers — especially heavyweights — appeared to be mutational throwbacks to Neanderthal Man, with limited powers of speech, and brains that had generally been reduced to a mushy paste through the thousands of punches which had been thrown around each encasing skull. Clay changed all that: of course, there were some eloquent fighters before, people who could string several words together in more or less coherent language. There were also some like-able personalities — and still are, for that matter. But the self-applauding, self-opinionated, egotistical, conceited, vain, blabbermouthing condescension of Cassius Clay — that was something new. It was also a publicist's dream. Before Cassius Clay came along, when the press said "Give us a few words, Champ", they got in reply several arcane low grunts, as though the boxer was preparing for a session of Primal Therapy, which were translated the following day as "The Champ says he will win", or "The Champ says he feels fine", although if anyone other than a professional boxer had uttered such sounds, they would have been rushed to hospital, and a call put out for a Transylvanian doctor. But with Cassius Clay, the press received enough verbatim copy to have their columns written for them — starting with the headline — and to publish a Clay supplement daily for as long as they wished.

The effect of this was to accrue to boxing the greatest amount of publicity it had received for many years. Suddenly, with the braggart, people outside of the sport took an interest in boxing. Many English people were enraged by Clay's boasting when he came to London for his first fight with Henry Cooper. Such people felt Clay's bragging was unsportsmanlike, disgraceful, and even *The Times* felt constrained to comment on Clay's manner, quoting Shakespeare in the process. Clay knew precisely what he was doing. He said later he got the idea two years before he first fought Henry Cooper, while on a visit to Las Vegas where he was to fight Duke Sabedong. During a television programme, a professional wrestler known as Gorgeous George came on and virtually took over the show, shouting how good he was, how dismal his opponent was, and how, with his hair having been carefully styled that day, he would commit all kinds of outrages if so much as a hair on his head was displaced. Like everyone else, Clay was intrigued by Gorgeous George, and faithfully watched the contest the following evening. The penny dropped. As it happened, Gorgeous George was a very good wrestler, and was rarely beaten, so the expectation of most members of the vast crowd which turned out to see the bout — the expectation of seeing him lose — was aroused more and more each time. To Cassius Clay, Gorgeous George's tactics seemed like a very good idea.

This could only happen in a sport or activity where the result left no room for argument: it could not have happened if the wrestler had been a symphonic conductor or an actor. The same kind of interest might have been aroused if a conductor went on television the night before a concert, stating that his performance of Beethoven's Fifth Symphony was going to be the greatest known to man. The actor, too, could boast about his 'Hamlet' before it happened. But they could never be the same as Ali's — or Gorgeous George's — bragging, for although Beethoven's Fifth is frequently beaten black and blue by ham-fisted conductors who are never on a jet plane long enough to study the music in peace and safety, there will always be a welter of published opinion which is almost impossible to disprove by objective fact. A performing artist cannot, under any circumstances, say what he likes without producing the opposite reaction. If anyone says he is good, then there is always going to be someone who will set out to prove he is not. In some ways, this is a good thing: truth is not the prerogative of any one person, and just as it is possible to become immune to the faults in one's self, or one's children, so blind hero-worship deserves the occasional cold douche. Some highly gifted people arouse antagonism in others, whereby the other person, sensing that someone is more gifted than they, will do all they can to discredit them, frequently using their position to harm their 'opponent'. In the end, however, the truth will out — it can never be entirely silenced, and something which is inherently good will always survive in some form, no matter if it takes many years for it to be recognised.

The reverse is often true: people are frequently praised for having qualities which they manifestly do not possess, but the truth of those matters, too, which have nothing to do with personalities, will eventually make itself known. The trouble is that this process can take a very long time, during which the people concerned will very likely grow old and die. This process of selection, of sifting the truth, *may* be democratic, but it is slow. What sport, and boxing in particular, offers, is a speeded-up version of the process. The moment of truth, in a fight, is not long in coming — we do not have to wait for future generations to deliver the verdict. Crystallised within sixty minutes at most, Muhammad Ali can be proved right or wrong in full view of everyone, and no-one can take that truth away.

If we went to a fight in order to see Muhammad Ali being beaten, we did so because a part of us said "I want to see him beaten because: he's got a big mouth/he's black/he's a Muslim/he's a coward/he knocked out Henry Cooper . . ." — in other words, there will always be a part of the audience which seeks revenge, for whatever reason. They cannot do it personally, so Ali's opponent becomes the personification of what they would like to do to him. All this has nothing to do with boxing. In the final chapter we will see how Ali's bragging has formed a part of his psychological weaponry, but for the moment we are concerned with his effect on the crowd. In this regard, the crowd has reacted against a man who has challenged assumptions, and forced them to think differently about a subject. They resent that, in the same way as they instinctively react against the forces of change when those forces seem loud and insistent. The extraordinary thing is that events have proved Muhammad Ali right: in a world where those who make the loudest noises tend to attract the most attention, Muhammad Ali has applied to boxing a tub-thumping manner familiar to anyone in advertising or politics. Like him or hate him, you could not ignore him.

Other reasons which go far beyond boxing with this man are his religious and political beliefs. They go hand in hand, for as a member of the Lost Found Nation of Islam (the Black Muslims), Muhammad Ali has embraced the teachings of the Honourable Elijah Muhammad. These teachings, which are somewhat unusual for many non-blacks to grasp, were imparted to Elijah Muhammad by the founder of the sect, a strange figure, Mr Farrad. Mr Farrad (one of several names used by the man) was a door-to-door silk salesman in Paradise Valley, a black ghetto in Detroit, during the 1930s. Mr Farrad gathered a small band of followers and preached of a lost heritage for black people. He vanished, as quickly and mysteriously as he appeared, but not before he implanted his teachings to his disciple Elijah Muhammad (formerly Poole), including a Gospel of 104 books, which remain unknown. The teachings encompass a view of history and astronomy which is certainly different, and foretell a destiny for black people — especially the blacks of America — which struck a responsive chord in those who suffered humiliation, deprivation and prejudice for many years. The story and teachings of this religious movement are quite outside the scope of this book. The Nation of Islam embraces a strict moral code, which discourages boxing, and Muhammad Ali is officially suspended while he fights. It should be remembered that Christian religions and Judaism came to be seen by militant blacks in the USA during the 1960s as essentially 'white-man's' religions. The attraction to an awakening dispossessed black population of a religious doctrine which ran counter to the established 'white' religions was considerable.

The reactions against it were also understandable. In the 1960s the civil rights movement, the ghetto riots and racial outbursts in major American cities demonstrated that the black man would no longer accept the status quo. When this was coupled with the growing involvement in a war in South-East Asia which was nightly splashed across the television screens of the United States — whose action in the war was unilateral — and which brought in its wake a growing demand to get out of that war coupled with a rejection of establishment standards by a large and articulate section of the country's youth, it was clear that sociologically the USA was in deep trouble. The public assassinations of its more enlightened leaders were symbols of that turmoil. When a black man, who was also a Black Muslim, *and* the Heavyweight Champion of the World, refused to be inducted into the United States Army, claiming his Muslim principles forbade it and saying "No Viet Cong ever called me a nigger", it was too much for many people. In a later chapter this is discussed in greater detail, in its chronological order, but ten years later it is curious to see that, with the Vietnam war long finished, the Nation of Islam has become the largest, wealthiest and strongest black organisation in the history of the USA, and has received the considerable financial support of people such as President Qaddafi of Libya. Without the public support of Muhammad Ali, it is doubtful if the movement would have become as big as it has done.

Another facet of Muhammad Ali's life has been his immense earning-power as a boxer — easily the wealthiest the world has seen. When he first turned professional, in 1960, he was managed by a consortium of Louisville businessmen, who had a six-year contract with him. Both sides valued the contract, and Ali has acknowledged the fair and honourable way in which he was treated by his backers. The contract expired shortly after one of the leading lights of the group, Bill Faversham, withdrew following two heart attacks. As Faversham was Ali's effective manager, and as Ali's growing association with the Black Muslims had made him a sensitive property to handle, it was natural that he should sign a contract with Herbert Muhammad, the son of Elijah Muhammad. Dundee remained Ali's trainer, and the new association was highly beneficial for all concerned. The main achievement of Herbert Muhammad was a remarkable escalation in Ali's earnings, as a glance at Appendix B will show. It is strange how the facts of Ali's life have conspired to work in his favour, for having been stripped of his title in 1967, there was naturally the keenest interest in a fight between Ali (who had not lost his title in the ring) and Joe Frazier (the acknowledged new champion) after Ali's return, in 1971. But even the highest-paid rock star must have blinked at the $2.5 million *each* fighter received for the contest. Even after that defeat, Ali commanded never less than $200,000 a fight, but his limit was easily exceeded first in 1974 in the world championship fight with George Foreman in Kinshasa (when Ali received over $5.4 million) and in 1975 for Ali's third meeting with Frazier in Manila, for which Ali received $6 million. This is big money by any standards, and is justified by the world interest in Ali. As all athletes have comparatively few years at the top, Herbert Muhammad's shrewd business affairs management has paid handsome dividends. It certainly made a change from the boxing 'organisations' of twenty or so years before.

A further point is Ali's travelling: he must surely be the most-travelled boxer in history, and has fought and defended his titles in many parts of the world. His Islamic faith has naturally led him to the emergent nations of Africa and Asia, and he has fought in places which had never seen a live world championship fight. In a very real sense, Muhammad Ali has been champion of the world, a refreshing change from other American title-holders who never once ventured outside the USA. This has been, generally speaking, all to the good. The most amazing example of Muhammad Ali's charismatic personality must be the fight against Foreman in Zaire: it took place at 3.00am, and 60,000 people turned up to see it. It is to be doubted if this would have happened in any of the more traditional boxing countries in the world.

There are other facets of this extraordinary man: his records, his Broadway appearance, his films, his television appearances, his autobiography. But all are part and parcel of the same thing — the life outside the ring of a great heavyweight fighter. All of these peripheral activities are interesting enough, but they would not mean a thing if Ali did not possess, first and foremost, the greatest and most complete boxing skill of all time. Muhammad Ali's exploits outside boxing have been written about on many occasions, but now let us turn out attention to the heart of the matter — his fights in the ring.

CHAPTER THREE

Beginnings

Cassius Marcellus Clay II was born on January 17th 1942, at the General Hospital, Louisville, Kentucky, USA. He was the eldest son of Cassius Marcellus Clay Sr, and Odessa Grady Clay, and weighed 6lbs 7ozs. Cassius Clay Sr was a signwriter who ran his own one-man business. Outside of his uncertain profession, which always managed to provide enough to support his family, if rarely more than that, Mr Clay liked to dabble in oils, specialising in landscapes and portraits. Something of a dreamer, perhaps, with an eye for a pretty girl, he occasionally turned to drink when the pressures got a little too much. This was easy in Louisville, the centre of a large whiskey distilling industry, but the liquor was sometimes too much for him to handle: on a couple of occasions he fell foul of the law. He always retained a justifiable pride in his financial independence, however, which was helped from time to time by the part-time cleaning jobs his wife occasionally took. Odessa Grady (her grandfather being an Irish O'Grady from County Clare), exerted a calming influence on the family. A non-smoker, non-drinker, and a devout Baptist, she made a point of her children observing good manners and behaviour at home. The family name had come down from General Cassius Marcellus Clay, a remarkable nineteenth-century plantation owner from Kentucky. General Clay was an early abolitionist, a noted politician (nominated for the vice-Presidency to run with Lincoln) and United States Ambassador. He was murdered by a gang of three youths in 1903 at the age of ninety-three, but not before his spirited defence of his life had included killing two of the attackers. When he set his slaves free, one of them took his name, which was passed on to the latest generations.

Young Cassius (his brother Rudolph was born two years later) was, by all accounts, a sturdy boy, quick and alert. His mother recalled that while still a babe in arms, he lashed out with his fist and dislodged one of her teeth, which had to be extracted by a local dentist. His appetite was immense, but he was a big child, not a fat one: when he was three years old, and still eligible for free travel on buses, the drivers insisted his mother paid his fare as he looked older and bigger than an average five-year-old.

The Clays lived at 3302 Grand Avenue, and, though money was never plentiful in the household, the twelve-year-old Cassius, a pupil of the DuValle Junior High School in Louisville, became the proud possessor of a new bicycle for Christmas, 'a Schwinn with red lights and chrome trim, a spotlight in the front, white wall tyres and chrome spikes and trims', which cost sixty dollars. Cassius received the bike some months before Christmas, and, naturally, was anxious to show it off in the neighbouhood. He recalled that when out riding one day with his best friend, Johnny Willis, heavy rain forced them to look for an indoor activity. They went to the annual Louisville Home Show, attracted by the free popcorn and hot-dogs on offer, but when it was time for the boys to leave, Cassius discovered that his bicycle had been stolen. He and his friend ran up and down several streets in a vain attempt to spot the bicycle, but it was no use. A passer-by saw the boy crying and, when told of the loss, directed Cassius to go down to the Columbia Gym (in the building where the Home Show had been held) to see Patrolman Joe Martin. It was the turning-point in Cassius Clay's life, for as he recalled in his autobiography:

". . . I ran downstairs, crying, but the sights and sounds and the smell of the boxing gym excited me so much that I almost forgot about the bike.

There were about ten boxers in the gym, some hitting the speed bag, some in the ring, sparring, some jumping rope. I stood there, smelling the sweat and rubbing alcohol, and a feeling of awe came over me . . ."

Martin ran the boxing gym in his spare time, and, after having taken particulars of the theft, he saw the interest in the young boy's eyes. He gave Cassius an application form to join the club, and the following Saturday, while at home watching television, Cassius saw a local amateur boxing show called *Tomorrow's Champions*. In a corner of the ring, with his protégé, was Joe Martin. From that moment, Cassius Clay wanted to be a boxer. He joined Joe Martin's gym, and spent every spare moment there. Naturally, Martin exerted a strong influence over the boy, and within a few weeks, on November 12th 1954, Cassius Clay fought his first amateur fight. His opponent was Ronnie O'Keefe, a white boy, whom he outpointed over three rounds on a split decision. As it happened, this first fight was televised on the *Tomorrow's Champions* show, and the young boxer's career could hardly have had more auspicious beginning.

Just across the way from the Columbia Gym is the Grace-Hope Community Centre, which also ran a youth boxing school, under a black coach, Fred Stoner. Cassius trained almost exclusively with Joe Martin in the early years, but occasionally with Fred Stoner, and under the watchful eyes of both men (who apparently had little in common other than their love of boxing) the young fighter developed his natural high ability.

At the age of fourteen, Cassius won his first Golden Gloves title, and set his sights on the national light-heavyweight title the following year. However, although he trained hard for it, and had built a growing reputation, during the medical examination before the fight an irregular heart murmur was diagnosed. Cassius had to withdraw, and Martin insisted he rest for four months, without doing any training. Whatever the condition was, it was evidently not serious, for it has never returned. Martin's insistence on a lay-off in training was undoubtedly the correct thing to do, but it must have caused great frustration to the young fighter. Martin's authoritarian methods stemmed from his policeman's discipline, and he recalled he often had to bring Cassius back into line over something or other, more than likely a remark the boy passed. Even at that early age, Cassius Clay had developed the habit of bragging about how good he was, and that one day he was going to be world champion. It was this attitude that upset the dour patrolman.

Cassius Clay won the Louisville Golden Gloves title in 1958 and proceeded to Chicago for the national tournament. He was defeated by Kent Green, and Ali recalls that this defeat — his first major loss — followed his first experience with a woman, the night before, so one assumes both encounters remain reasonably strong memories. Ali blamed his loss on the woman, but it was a temporary setback. His wins continued, and by the following year he had avenged his defeat, this time definitely beating Tony Madigan to lift the national Golden Gloves light-heavyweight championship. Clay's self-confidence had already led him to introduce himself to Angelo Dundee, the noted trainer, when Dundee visited Louisville with the fighter Willie Pastrano, who was matched against George Holman. Clay called on Dundee and Pastrano at their hotel, and, with becoming modesty, claimed that he was going to become heavyweight champion of the world. He persuaded Dundee to agree to a sparring bout with Pastrano at the gym the following day, but the bout was stopped before the end of round one, Ali claiming that this was due to his superior speed and jabbing.

As Cassius's success continued, so did his self-confidence. He explained to fellow-boxer José Torres:

". . . When I started fighting seriously, I found out that grown people, the fight fans, acted like the school kids of my day. Almost from the first fights, I'd mouth off to anybody who would listen about what I was going to do to whoever I was going to fight. People would go out of their way to come and see me, hoping I would get beat. When I was no more than a kid fighter, they would put me in bills because I was a drawing-card, because I run my mouth so much. Other kids could battle and get all bloody and lose or win and didn't hardly anybody care, it seemed like, except me, maybe their families, and their buddies.

But the minute I would come in sight, people would start hollering, 'Bash in his nose!' or 'Button his fat lip!' or something like that. I didn't care what they said long as they kept coming to see me fight. They paid their money, they was entitled to a little fun. You would have thought I was some well-known pro, ten years older than I was . . ."

Although this was some years before he encountered Georgeous George, there was clearly nothing anyone could tell the young fighter about publicity, but he also had the ability to go with it. In May 1959, Cassius lost to Amos Johnson in the finals of the Pan-American Games: it was a significant defeat, for it stopped an unbroken record of 36 consecutive wins, and Johnson was a southpaw. Cassius found it difficult to cope with the 'opposite' stance and attack. It was also Cassius's last amateur defeat, and the months following showed Joe Martin to have his eyes — and those of his protégé — set on the Olympic Games, to be held in Rome in 1960.

By February of that year Cassius had won his sixth Kentucky Golden Gloves title, and the next month he was with his brother Rudolph (who had also joined the Martin stable) in Chicago to compete again in the champion's tournament, but fighting as a heavyweight in order that he would not have to fight against his brother, who was fighting as a light-heavyweight. On to New York, where at Madison Square Garden he defeated Gary Jawish by a knockout in the third round. In April he participated in the AAU championship, retaining his national title by a technical knockout in round two. His unprecedented run of success meant he was a foregone conclusion for selection in the Olympic team, but to make doubly sure he entered the Eastern Regional Olympic qualifying bouts in Louisville in April, and won all three of his fights by technical knockouts. The following month, despite a fear of flying, Cassius attended the Olympic Trials at Cow Palace, San Francisco, and won his ticket to Rome after winning all his three bouts, the third a particularly fine win over the Army champion, Allen Hudson. Cassius was somewhat disconcerted by Hudson's extraordinary habit of talking during the fight, which might have contributed to a Hudson punch which floored Cassius in round one. The fight was stopped in round three after a flurry of punches from Clay. Hudson's tactic of speaking to his opponent during the fight made a more lasting impression on Cassius than his punch. His fear of flying had not been overcome by the trip to San Francisco, and he returned home by train, a long and laborious journey. On April 18th, he had registered for military service, on reaching the age of eighteen years, three months.

When the United States Olympic Party arrived in Rome in July 1960, the official light-heavyweight representative was at his most ebullient. Without the restraining influence of Joe Martin, or Fred Stoner, or his mother, Cassius Clay was thrilled to be in the Eternal City, with a golden opportunity in front of him. He lost no time in making sure everyone knew of his intentions. Within a few days, his boasting and bragging made him one of the most notorious figures in Olympic Village, and the press and other media personnel were soon flocking to hear his latest predictions. Some of the fellow-athletes found his manner unacceptable, and not at all in the true Olympic spirit, but Cassius meant no harm. He was in the position of a child being given the run of

10

a fantastic toyshop, and he was in his element. He certainly showed the other athletes how to enjoy life, but his training, which on occasion showed signs of slacking, did not really suffer: he took the occasional talking-to in good part, and they sensed, underneath his outward show of flamboyance, that he realised the seriousness of the task before him.

His first fight, against the Belgian Yvon Becaus was stopped in round two to save the Belgian from further punishment, but his second fight, against the Russian Gennady Shatkov was not so easy, for the Russian's experience was much greater than that of Becaus. However, in round three Clay pulled ahead, and outpointed Shatkov in a fine win.

He was now in the semi-finals, and his opponent was the Australian Tony Madigan whom he had fought before. It was a close decision, as Madigan was a determined and resourceful fighter, but Clay's speed of attack enabled him to land a considerable number of scoring punches in the final round, which must have just tipped the scales in the American's favour. Cassius Clay had reached the Olympic finals.

Clay and his Polish opponent, Zbigniew 'Ziggy' Piertrzkowski, had to wait a further two weeks for their bout, held on September 15th in the Palazzo dello Sport. Clay trained hard, for he knew that the Pole was a southpaw, and he had always experienced difficulty against the unorthodox stance of right-leading boxers. In addition, Piertrzkowski was a vastly more experienced boxer than Cassius, and had won the bronze medal in the previous Olympic Games, in Melbourne in 1956.

In the event the fight proved more one-sided than many imagined it would be: the Polish fighter had clearly heard of Cassius's reputation, and began slowly, with Clay himself as usual a little disconcerted by the awkward approach of his opponent. By all accounts, half-way through round two, Clay had begun to overcome the difficulty, and was soon landing a succession of punches of devastating power and accuracy. In the third, final, round, it was all-Clay: a whirlwind of activity which left the Pole's face badly cut and mauled, with blood almost literally all over his face from multiple cuts sustained against Clay's persistent blows to his eyes, nose and mouth. The fight should have been stopped before the bell, but Clay had won easily. He was now the Olympic champion, the possessor of a gold medal, and his pride became overbearing with an 'I told you so' self-confidence that stuck in the throats of some losers.

After a brush with a Russian reporter, during which he answered a leading question with a remarkable degree of skill and choice turn of phrase, Cassius Clay flew home, first to New York, where Joe Martin was at the airport to meet him. Martin already had people clamouring after Cassius, one of the more significant being a millionaire tobacco baron, William Reynolds, who put up Cassius for several days at the Waldorf-Astoria, while the young champion went on a rubber-necking sightseeing trip. After a relaxing few days in New York, discussing the offer of Mr Reynolds with Joe Martin, and picking up presents for his family, Cassius and Joe returned to Louisville.

Back in his native city, Cassius Clay was accorded a tremendous civic reception. He stepped from the plane at Louisville airport, wearing his medal, to the delight of the crowd assembled to welcome him — and his parents, especially his mother, who was the first to rush up and kiss her son. For Cassius Clay Sr, it was the first time he had publicly shown an interest in his son's career, and he must have been as impressed as his son was at the motorcade which took them to a reception at Central High. The young boxer had a twenty-five car police escort on the journey downtown. At the school where Cassius had previously not done very well in his academic subjects, tending to daydream about boxing, there were greetings from the Governor of Kentucky, and the Mayor told Cassius the medal effectively gave him the freedom of the city. When confronted by a large, cheering crowd, the blabbermouth was lost for words, momentarily humbled by the warmth and humanity of the genuine popular feelings of pride and pleasure at his success.

Shortly afterwards, Cassius went to the mayor's office with a friend, riding his new motor-bike, to show the olympic medal to a group of dignitaries who were visiting the city. After the usual polite noises from the mayor, it became clear that Cassius's remark to the Russian reporter had been taken for rather more than was meant. The Russian had questioned Clay pointedly on racial prejudice, and the young man's spirited defence of America was taken by many conservatives as an endorsement of all aspects of the American way of life. Cassius realised that any attempt to 'correct' his remark would doubtless be further misinterpreted, and he left the mayor's office, as he recalled, "resolved that if I could not change my remark before the public, I would change it for myself."

Later that afternoon, with his friend in tow, Cassius stopped by a local hamburger joint for a snack. He was refused service as he was black. There followed a dramatic confrontation, and not even Cassius's Olympic medal could get him his food. He was forced to leave, and was followed by several trouble-makers. It was evening, and Cassius drove to the Ohio River, where the Jefferson County Bridge spans it, and, after a brief but vicious fight with his pursuers, he was so disgusted by what had happened that he stood in the centre of the bridge and tore the Olympic medal from his neck. He flung it far out into the current, where it lies to this day, buried in the mud at the bottom of the river.

A day or so before, a Louisville businessman, Bill Faversham, who followed Cassius's career with interest, had learned that the boxer had decided to reject the proposition of Mr Reynolds as negotiated by Joe Martin. Although it was a fair and reasonable offer, the boxer's father advised against becoming managed by a policeman. Cassius had nothing against Joe for being a policeman (perhaps his father's occasional brushes with the law had coloured his advice) but felt the patrolman lacked the necessary experience and business acumen to make a notable mark in the demanding world of boxing management.

Bill Faversham had formed a consortium of eleven leading Louisville businessmen, and his offer was an extremely attractive one for the fighter, with shrewd clauses calling for a percentage of his earnings to be earmarked for a pension fund, not to be touched until Cassius reached the age of thirty-five. It also offered a $10,000 non-recoverable advance on signing.

The decision did not require much thought. It could hardly be haggled over, and gave the young boxer the best possible start on a commercial footing. On October 26th 1960, in the presence of his admiring parents, Cassius Clay signed the contract. He was now a fully professional boxer.

CHAPTER FOUR

On the Road

With part of his $10,000 advance, Cassius bought a pink Cadillac for his parents, and, three days after signing with the Louisville Sporting Group (as Bill Faversham's consortium was called), Cassius made his debut as a professional fighter, in a match against Tunney Hunsaker. This had been fixed up before he signed with the consortium, and his purse was a respectable $2,000. His performance was also respectable, having trained assiduously under Fred Stoner's watchful eye. His brother Rudy was his sparring partner. The fight took place in Louisville's Freedom Hall, and pulled in 6,000 spectators, eager to see the local boy on his first outing.

As José Torres has pointed out, there is always a fascination for the first professional fight of a boxer who goes on to become a great champion. Joe Louis, Floyd Patterson, Rocky Marciano and Joe Frazier — and José Torres — all won their debut fights by knockouts. A boxer's first professional fight should have him all keyed up, anxious to show what he is made of. It is curious that, although Cassius Clay won his first fight comparatively easily, it was no knockout, but a points decision over six rounds against a part-time boxer who was a full-time sheriff. Faversham, apparently, was not terribly impressed by Clay's first outing, and felt some rigorous training with Archie Moore, who ran a boxing camp known as the Salt Mine outside San Diego, was called for. Consequently, Cassius left for California, and knuckled down to work. Moore was deeply impressed by Clay, saying he had "utterly astounding potential", but the two men were not temperamentally suited. Moore, like Joe Martin, was not enamoured of Clay's arrogance and insistence on doing things his way. Cassius trained hard with Moore, but would not accept orthodox instruction. It was clear they could not get on together, and Clay returned to Louisville, with a problem for Faversham. However, Faversham had been at work, and the name of Angelo Dundee was put forward. Faversham met Dundee at the latter's training quarters on Fifth Street in Miami, and eventually Dundee — after expressing enthusiasm for the chance to work with Clay — got the job as his trainer. Clay was so anxious to begin that he missed Christmas at home in order to start work immediately with Dundee. Impressed by Clay's dedication, a fight was arranged on December 27th in Miami Beach against Herb Siler. Willie Pastrano was also on the bill, headlining it against Jesse Bawdry. Cassius's fight lasted four rounds before he knocked out Siler with a right to the body and a left hook to the jaw. It was certainly an improvement over his first professional decision.

Shortly after New Year 1961, Clay fought three more bouts within 36 days, all in Miami. On January 17th (his nineteenth birthday) Clay stopped Tony Esperti in three rounds; on February 7th in the Miami Convention Hall he scored a clean knockout against Jim Robinson within two minutes of round one, and finally, on February 21st, against his first notably experienced professional opponent, Donnie Fleeman, a fine win in round seven.

The fight with Fleeman was an eight-round bout, and would doubtless have gone the full distance, owing to Fleeman's experience and stamina, had it not been for Clay's speed and incessant jabbing, which cut Fleeman so badly that the referee had to end the fight one round early. Of Fleeman's 51 fights, he had won 45 of them, 20 by knocking out his opponent, so Clay's win was very impressive. Clay was impatient to get on: every day at the gym he would badger Dundee to let him box and not just train. He got his way, and in the process a lot of experience, for Dundee recalled the older pro boxers would give Clay a hard time to shut him up, but he soon showed his mettle by being able to handle anything that was thrown at him.

In April Faversham fixed up a fight between Cassius and Lamar Clark, back home in Louisville, and Clay travelled there with the trainer. Clark, a farmer from Utah, had a remarkable record — much more impressive than Fleeman's had been. Clark's particular habit was knocking people out: his last 45 consecutive opponents had been stopped in this way, and Cassius Clay was not going to upset this string of victories. But the hometown boy had other ideas, and, with an arrogance that must have surprised those who thought they knew him well, Cassius said *he* was going to knock Clark out — in two rounds. This was Cassius's first professional prediction. The fight took place in Fairground Coliseum before 5,400 spectators, most of whom, it is safe to assume, were there to see Clay get himself spanked.

Clay came out like a whirlwind, and battered Clark so frequently that he soon broke the farmer's nose. In round two he floored Clark three times before, in front of the astonished gaze of the onlookers, he delivered the killer blow which knocked Clark out. His prediction had come true. It is not difficult to imagine the reaction afterwards: the press crowded round Clay, eager for quotes, and the young boxer, with a nonchalant air, as if to imply "what's all the fuss about?" simply said, "I just had the feeling he must fall". They had never heard — or seen — anything like it.

After resting at home for a while, Clay returned to Miami, a little overweight from his mother's cooking, to prepare for his next fight, this time in Las Vegas, against Kolo 'Duke' Sabedong. This was a different proposition: it was Cassius's first ten-round fight, and Sabedong, who at 6ft 6ins stood several inches taller than Cassius, and at 16st (226lbs) was no pushover, being significantly heavier. Clay was more worried about the flight to Vegas, but once there, and having seen Gorgeous George for the first time, Clay had no trouble. Sabedong, for all his weight, had lost 12 of his 27 fights — rather too many for comfort — and his lumbering style seemed oddly inappropriate against Clay's fleet manner. Inappropriate or not, he survived the ten rounds with Clay, who won on points.

Back home in Louisville, after a particularly hazardous return flight which did nothing to assuage Clay's nervousness of planes, Cassius prepared for his next fight. This took place on July 22nd, and was televised live. His adversary was his first ranked heavyweight opponent, Alonzo Johnson, who — somewhat predictably — went the full ten rounds with Cassius, but — rather less predictably — won only one of those rounds, with Clay taking the remaining nine. Angelo Dundee later said:

"... His improvement from his previous Sabedong fight was impressive. Johnson was a better fighter than Sabedong, but this time Clay boxed smart and was able to connect with clean punches. I thought he was ready for the big leagues ..."

However Dundee felt about his fighter's ability, he waited a while longer before allowing Cassius a bite at the big cherry. Ten weeks after beating Johnson, a good period of time to wind down, build his strength, and wind up again, Clay was matched to fight Alex Miteff, also in Louisville. For this bout, Cassius was again predicting an early win: "He'll go in six," he foretold, but in round two, Miteff almost stopped the young fighter in his tracks with a right cross to the jaw which had everyone worried — except Miteff. For the first time in his professional career, Cassius Clay looked to be in trouble momentarily, but the moment of truth for Dundee came as Cassius shook off the attack, and the effects of the punch, and came back more strongly against his opponent. It was clear that his insistence on continual boxing in Dundee's Fifth Street Gym had taught him to take punishment as well as being able to dish it out.

From the third round onwards, it was all Cassius, and in the sixth, he hit Miteff incessantly until the referee closed the curtains on the Argentinian. Clay had done it again.

On November 29th, Clay was back again in Louisville for his third successive fight in his home town. His opponent was a German, Willie Besmanoff, whose thick, impacted features were impressive. However, this fight marked Besmanoff's return to the ring after a six-month lay-off and he was naturally angry at some highly derogatory 'Gorgeous George' remarks from Cassius on a local television show. His abuse was pretty strong:

"... I'm embarrassed to get in the ring with this unrated duck — I'm ready for top contenders ... Besmanoff must fall in seven ..."

Not *quite* ready for the world's greatest heavyweights, thought Dundee, but after his good wins over Johnson and Miteff, this outing with Besmanoff seemed hardly a step forward for Clay.

When the bell rang for round one, Besmanoff came out, full of fire and speed, rushing at Clay. He was so screwed up that his anger quite literally got the better of him, for Clay was able to duck and weave away from the German's slinging throws, and in retaliation landed successions of combinations to the bewildered Besmanoff's face. It was clear that Clay could have put his opponent away from round five onwards, when by all accounts Besmanoff appeared defenceless, but perhaps because he wanted to make his prediction come true, Cassius tended to play with his opponent and string out the match, ignoring Dundee's ringside pleas to finish the German off. This was the first time, but certainly not the last, when Clay exhibited traces of arrogance in the ring, playing with his man, not seizing chances, confident of his ability to finish the match in his own good time, when *he* was good and ready and not before. In round seven, the round called by Clay, the Louisville boy unleashed an impressive array of jabs and punches, concluding with a right to the German's jaw. Besmanoff went down for the second time in the round, this time backwards, helpless, and lay absolutely immobile for a long time — a little over ten seconds. Apparently, the referee did not even bother to count the German out — it was all over, and another prediction had come true.

Now people really began talking about Cassius Clay: the new year, 1962, dawned and an unexpected opportunity arose for him to appear at the boxing court of the USA at that time — Madison Square Garden, New York City. This would be his first professional fight in that prestigious venue. A scheduled bout was cancelled at five days notice between two rated heavyweights, and Dundee was asked if it would be possible for Clay to fight a substitute bout there, against Sonny Banks. After a quick consultation, Dundee agreed, and Clay lost little time in using advantage of an engagement, as guest of the New York Boxing Writers' Association monthly dinner, the Wednesday before the bout, to predict the outcome of the fight. "The man must fall in the round I call — in fact, Banks must fall in four." The die was cast. The New York fight was another big chance for Clay, who came out in a completely unorthodox manner, surprising the hard-bitten Manhattan fight fans by dancing around Banks with his arms down by his side. Banks caught him suddenly, and Clay went down, obliged to take a mandatory count of eight. When the fight resumed, it was a different Clay — minus the Keystone Kops style. The next two rounds were more straightforward, and at the start of the fateful fourth, Clay came out, all-action, as in the seventh against Besmanoff. He overwhelmed Banks, so much so that Banks was unable to do anything to prevent the knockout blow. Once again, the prediction proved correct, but not without a fright in round one.

Perhaps that rash miscalculation by Clay caused Dundee to have second thoughts before allowing his fighter back in the important venue. In any event, Clay was scheduled to meet his next opponent, Don Warner, in Miami Beach on February 28th, at the Auditorium. Clay appearently indulged in more predictions — round five this time, but in the event he blasted Warner out in the fourth round. When asked why he had not made his prediction come true, Cassius replied that he felt he had to penalise Warner, who had not shaken hands with him at the weigh-in. According to José Torres, Clay could have taken Warner earlier, but chose to carry him.

The next fight was on the West Coast: in Los Angeles, the legendary Joe Louis, now turned boxing promoter, matched Clay against George Logan. Clay's takings from the fight were over $9,000 — easily his biggest fee up to then — and it was comparatively easy money, for all Logan's much-vaunted left hook, as Clay, Torres reported, "made Logan's hands look silly". Clay was much in demand, naturally, from the local media, and left Los Angeles a much more famous person than when he arrived, his prediction of a round four win again justified by the technical knockout.

Less than a month later, Clay was back in New York, to meet a man somewhat similar to himself. Like Clay, Billy Daniels was a young black fighter, with a growing and impressive ring record, a local boy much favoured by the press. There the resemblance ended, for Daniels was not in the same class as Clay: there was much holding and pushing, unattractive for the spectators, and frustrating for Clay. In round seven, however, his attrition-like offensive against Daniels paid off, for the referee stopped the fight in Clay's favour, anxious to prevent the cut on Daniels's face from getting worse. Up to then, it had been a close fight, with Daniels's tactics preventing Clay from getting into his stride.

Having fought Warner on February 28th, Logan on April 23rd and Daniels on May 19th, Clay's engagement book needed some blank pages, and it was not until July 20th that he was again in Los Angeles, to meet Alejandro Lavorante. Murmurings had already been made for Clay to move up into the big time, with a proposed meeting against Archie Moore sometime before the end of 1962: Moore was living out-side Los Angeles, and attended the Lavorante match. He saw a remark-able fight. Lavorante was a little over the hill, but in his day had been a world-ranked heavyweight contender, and had tremendous experience at the very top of the profession. In round one, Lavorante landed two powerful punches to Clay's body, which shook the younger man, but, coming back in the second, it was Clay who caught Lavorante's jaw with a right cross of considerable venom. Lavorante, an Argentinian, was virtually finished from that moment on, as Clay set about demolishing him. Lavorante's eyes were both cut, and his face was badly battered, before he was felled twice in round four. In the fifth round, the one in which Clay had predicted the Argentinian would go, a powerful right hand from the Louisville boy completely floored Lavorante, who had nothing left to offer. Yet another of Clay's predictions had come true, and for many people, this young braggart was getting a little too big for his boots. A large part of the audience would have dearly loved to see the Mouth silenced, but at the end of the fight, in the milling around the ring, Clay caught Archie Moore's eye, down by the ringside. He called out to the veteran: "You're next, Archie!" And again, "You're next, old man!"

Lavorante fought only one more fight: a few months after having been beaten by Clay, he lost to Johnny Riggens. It was one of boxing's rare tragedies: Lavorante's brain was seriously damaged in the fight, and he collapsed into a coma from which he never recovered. After nineteen months in a comatose state, Lavorante died in April 1964.

But for Cassius Clay, Archie Moore was indeed to be the next opponent. After 21 months as a professional heavyweight boxer, having fought 15 fights, and won all 15, 12 by knockouts, the Big Time had arrived.

CHAPTER FIVE

The Big Time

(1)
November 15th 1962
v ARCHIE MOORE (USA)
venue: Los Angeles Sports Arena
Cassius Clay: 14st 8lbs (204lbs)
Archie Moore: 14st 11lbs (207lbs)
Referee: Tommy Hart
Attendance: 16,000

Before Cassius Clay could be considered a worthy contender for a crack at Sonny Liston's world title, he had to show his prowess over a better class of boxer than he had beaten thus far. Clay's record was impressive: he had won his first fifteen professional bouts, 12 within the distance — and the previous seven fights had all been knockout victories. It was right for him to have his eyes set on the heavyweight championship of the world, but he still had some way to go. Lavorante had been his most important contestant up until the fight with Moore, and Clay was rated ninth in the world before the Moore fight.

It was this fight which put Clay resolutely on the map in big-time world boxing. His brash manner was put down to his impetuous youthfulness, and his doggerel "Archie Moore will go in four", attracted attention and needled the old pro.

Moore was one of the most incredible boxers of all time. He began his professional career in 1936, six years before Cassius Clay was born, and had fought over 220 bouts before he met Clay — 135 of these fights had been won by Moore through knockouts. No-one knew exactly how old he was (for that matter, no one knew how old Sonny Liston was), but he must have been close to fifty at the time of this fight. He had been light-heavyweight champion of the world for the previous ten years, before being 'stripped' of his title for a paltry reason. He was still rated fifth in the world in the heavyweight league.

The fight was postponed for three weeks owing to poor gate receipts, but in that breathing-space both boxers (Moore less than Clay) did all they could to whip up enthusiasm for the battle. Clay's insulting attitude towards the elderly boxer did the trick for the gate money was $182,599, of which Clay took $45,300 — easily his biggest purse, and three times that which he got for beating Lavorante. A year before, Clay was making between two to six thousand dollars a fight. He had come a long way in a short time.

Whatever good intentions Moore had of "shutting that fresh boy's mouth", Moore soon learned that the road to hell is paved with them. From the opening bell Clay dominated the fight, and it was crystal-clear that Moore was physically incapable of doing what his brain told him to do. Moore was paunchy, greying, and leaden-footed. In comparison, Clay was the sweet bird of youth — the epitome of young physical excellence. To be fair, Clay's speed doubtless made Moore appear slower than he was, for Moore must have expected the 'usual' kind of heavyweight opponent. But for Clay, there was no lumbering around the ring: Moore's reflexes were unable to cope with the young dynamo.

In round two, the onslaught continued against Moore, but he had not been fighting over a quarter of a century for nothing: he sized Clay up, and caught him with an immensely powerful right to Clay's body which clearly hurt the younger man. Clay backed off, recovering from this herculean punch, but only momentarily: he returned to the fray, his left jabs flying out and gradually making the ageing boxer's face appear marked and scored. All Moore could do was to weave and duck out of harm's way, but he was quite unable to get out of the way of Clay's combination punches, which literally had him reeling. The end was in sight, and when the bell for round four sounded, the round in which Clay had said Moore must go, the tension and excitement had been raised to a high degree. Clay attacked again unmercifully: a stunning left and right sent the old-timer down for a count of eight. Moore heaved himself up just in time. Clay again attacked, and within seconds Moore was down once more. Unwilling to grant Clay the fulfilment of his round four prediction, Moore again gamely struggled to his feet, but was only able, once the bout continued, to stand shuffling in the centre of the ring, his hands clasped around his head to withstand Clay's combinations. A left hook from Clay, followed by a vicious right, caught the old man's head, and sent him again to the floor. This was the end as far as the referee was concerned, for Tommy Hart stepped between them and signalled it was all over.

Moore got to his feet, and walked out of the ring by himself. It was his swansong in big fights: he had acquitted himself as well as he could, but for Clay it was a fine win nearer to the ultimate title. After the fight, Moore paid Clay a great compliment: "He is an excellent boxer . . . I didn't think he was so good."

(2)
January 24th 1963
v CHARLIE POWELL (USA)
venue: Pittsburgh Civic Arena
Cassius Clay: 14st 9lbs (205lbs)
Charlie Powell: 15st 4lbs (214lbs)
Referee: Ernie Sesto
Attendance: 17,000

Having disposed of Archie Moore, Cassius Clay soon found his name
on everyone's lips — it was not exactly overnight fame, but it was a big
stepping-stone in his career. Not for the first time, and not for the last,
had a highly talented, eager young boxer beaten a much older man.
Moore had under-rated Clay, but Clay's attraction for the man in the
street was clearly demonstrated with his next fight. Powell was an ex-
professional football player, who had turned heavyweight boxer. He did
not figure in the top ratings, and had pursued a somewhat mediocre
career as a fighter. Essentially, therefore, the fight appeared to be a
public workout for Clay, whose career would not be advanced one iota
by a defeat of Powell. However, it kept Clay in trim, and his name
before the public. Ordinarily, a fight between Charlie Powell and an
up-and-coming heavy-weight would not have rated highly on many
boxing fans lists of tasty encounters, but Clay surprised his promoters
by his charisma which was already able to attract a very large crowd to
see him fight. To the astonishment of many boxing experts, 17,000
people turned out on a wintry night (the temperature reportedly 20
degrees below zero) to see Clay fight. Clay, like before with Moore, had
indulged in a little pre-fight predicting, when he said he would knock
Powell out in round three.

The fight began as though preordained: Clay, quickly dancing
around Powell, jabbing him, early on, and doing so with great agility
and dispatch. The hapless Powell seemed bemused by the scurrying
urgency of Clay, being unable to land a decent punch at all, often
missing Clay completely, appearing flat-footed and hopelessly outclassed in the process. Those punches of Powell that did land appeared
to do so largely through luck, but they troubled Clay not a jot, as he
continued on his light-footed, animated way.

The round was clearly Clay's and again in round two Powell was
thrown *in medias res* at the centre of Clay's restlessness. Powell was no
calm at the hub of the whirlwind, but a fighter always on the defensive,
not knowing where the next attack was coming from, and completely
unable to mount any kind of retaliatory action. Powell was not only
being hit often — he was being hit hard, and it seemed towards the end
of round two that Clay's prediction would come all too true in the third.
And so it did: early in the round, Clay advanced on the luckless Powell,

piling combinations in and around his head and body, forcing him back onto the ropes, from which position, with Powell ducking in instinctive defence from Clay's scorching attack, Clay delivered the killer-blow. A vicious right, straight to Powell's head, sent him finally sprawling to the safety of the canvas, where he was counted out.

(3)
March 16th 1963
v DOUG JONES (USA)
venue: Madison Square Garden, New York City
Cassius Clay: 14st 6lbs (202lbs)
Doug Jones: 13st 6lbs (188lbs)
Referee: Joe LoScalzo
Attendance: 18,732

By now, Clay's nine consecutive knockouts in his seventeen-bout professional career had set the boxing world buzzing with interest at the dynamic young boxer. Clay's eyes were firmly set on the world title, and, following his victory against Archie Moore, he was now rated second in the world. It was only natural, therefore, that he should be matched against other contenders, and this fight against Doug Jones (who was rated third) attracted considerable attention.

In the event, it was a closer fight than Clay imagined it would be. He had predicted a fourth round knockout, but this was before the weigh-in, which Clay attended with a large sticking-plaster spread across his mouth. Naturally, publicity followed, and, almost inevitably, there were those eager to see the young orator stopped.

The opening round was notable for both boxers attacking fast and furiously, with little finesse, and neither seeming to take the trouble to weigh up the characteristics of the other. At least, that's how it appeared, but Jones got first blood — not literally, however — by catching Clay with several strong combination punches. This only served to stimulate Clay, whose speed and agility were already the talk of boxing, to a furious retaliation. The number of Clay's punches was easily double that of Jones, and they landed accurately, almost exclusively, to the head.

If your aim is to knock out a fighter, then head shots are called for, and Clay, by attacking Jones's head incessantly — hardly landing a blow on his opponent's body — clearly meant to realise his prediction. The first law of boxing is to defend yourself, but Clay's method of doing this was decidedly unorthodox — if not dangerous in many people's eyes. Clay was so anxious to beat Jones in four rounds that in the opening part of the bout little of Clay's speedy footwork was in evidence. He attempted to stand and slug it out with Jones, but after round four, when it was clear his prediction was not to be, Clay changed his tactics. His punches, however, were still amazingly fast up to the end of the fourth in his determined effort to beat Jones, but after that it was as though he had begun a second fight. Clay's changes in style and manner were surprising. He began to bob and weave, jab and push, peppering Jones's face while searching for an opening.

Jones, however, had other ideas: he gave Clay an object-lesson in classical defensive boxing when under attack, for he never offered the young Kentuckian a chance. As the bout progressed, Clay appeared to tire much more quickly than Jones — an indication of the effort he had put into the first four rounds. Jones came back at Clay very strongly in the seventh and eighth rounds. But Clay was not to be thwarted — he still had his ambition to fulfil, and with a determined effort, which showed part of his true character, Clay fought back on top in the final rounds, taking the fight all the time to Jones, and staggering him more than once with tremendous right crosses. Jones, however, refused to go down, and denied Clay the knockout he clearly wanted. At the bell, with both men steadfastly on their feet, swapping punch for punch, it was the unanimous decision of both judges and the referee that gave the verdict to Clay.

It was a good win — not as commanding as Clay would have hoped — but a slight curiosity was the variance in the scoring. Both ringside judges gate the fight to Clay 5-4-1, but the referee thought Clay had won much more convincingly, 8-1-1. Perhaps being in such close proximity to the fighters meant that LoScalzo could appreciate the speed and effectiveness of Clay's dazzling combinations. But, as Winston Churchill said of majorities, "one is enough", and Clay had achieved his victory.

(4)
June 18th 1963
v HENRY COOPER (GREAT BRITAIN)
venue: Empire Stadium, Wembley
Cassius Clay: 14st 11lbs (207lbs)
Henry Cooper: 13st 3½lbs (185½lbs)
Referee: T Little
Attendance: 50,000

Henry Cooper, the British and Empire Heavyweight Champion, then twenty-nine, had just won convincingly over the Welshman, Dick Richardson, and was the best-loved British boxer then active in the ring. Cooper's straightforward honesty and integrity had endeared him to many people, and Clay could not have done more to upset the British crowd than he did by calling Cooper a cripple — and much more. "This ain't no jive — Henry Cooper will fall in five", boasted Clay, and the

24

British crowd were keen to see Cooper win. Much was made of Cooper's vulnerable eyebrows, but in fact damage to them had only resulted in a couple of his defeats in an impressive career.

Clay, however, at twenty-one, had several distinct advantages: he was eight years younger, fifteen to twenty pounds heavier, was one inch taller than Cooper, and had several inches longer in reach. Perhaps most important of all, Clay had the fastest hands of any heavyweight in the world. His whiplash left jabs, in staccato repetition, plus his punishing rights to the head were part of his greater versatility than Cooper's more traditional arsenal. Clay held his hands low, and relied on his footwork to keep him out of trouble. If, however, his attention were to falter fractionally for Cooper to land his left hook, then Clay could very well find himself in trouble. In addition, Cooper was on home ground: the crowd was behind him all the way, and his likeable personality had won him the respect and admiration of countless thousands of his fellow-Britishers.

As it turned out, the fight was possibly the best performance of Cooper's career, and contained moments of high drama and excitement. Most people thought Clay would win, *if* he could keep away from Cooper's left, and Clay himself, sensing the value of publicity, was already itching to grab at Liston's crown. A decisive win, and he would be one step nearer the match with Liston. For some people, Clay was already world champion clown, and he startled the vast crowd by appearing at the ringside wearing a cardboard crown. Cooper was undeterred: the two men had no personal animosity, and actually a close rapport had sprung up between them, but from the moment the bell sounded, its clamour dimly perceived through the tumultuous noise of the crowd, the fight was on in deadly earnest.

Whoever had been keeping tabs on Clay for Cooper had obviously done his homework: within ten seconds Cooper took the fight to Clay, demonstrating both the speed and power of his left hand. Clay appeared faintly surprised at Cooper's opening, and the crowd, sensing that Cooper meant this fight in deadly seriousness, began a roar of the two syllables, "Coo-per, Coo-per," urging their champion on. Within the first minute, Cooper landed three sharp left jabs, and two left hooks to the head. Already Clay appeared to seek the defence of extensive holding, and in fact the second left hook from Cooper cut Clay. Referee Little, on a break, warned Clay for holding, and this admonition raised the temperature of the crowd several degrees. They sensed an upset, but the clinches became too frequent for their liking. Another clinch, late in the round, caused Clay to protest to the referee that it was Cooper holding this time: why not warn the British boxer, too? But referee Little would have none of it, and soon the bell brought the opening round to an end.

The first round quite clearly belonged to Cooper, and everyone knew it: Clay's seconds worked quickly to patch up the facial damage, and the bleeding troubled him no more. At the start of the second round, Clay lolloped out his mouth drooping open in mock disbelief at Cooper's determination and success. This ploy meant nothing to Cooper: catching Clay before the American could escape, he hit Clay with one, two and three stunning left jabs to the face. Cooper's power was there for all to see and for Clay to feel, and people round the ringside could not really believe that Clay, the great 'jab-and-run' exponent, was being beaten at his own game. The three left jabs stung Clay: deep down inside he knew he would not win this fight on points by dancing and clinching — he had to hit Cooper. A couple of shots to Cooper's head got through, but Cooper retaliated with some good left jabs and, unusually, intelligent scoring with his right. Towards the two-minute period, Clay's occasional shots to Cooper's head paid off: ominously, blood appeared below Cooper's left eye, a nick had been opened, and the dreams of the British crowd took a sharp downturn as the blood became visible. Surely not again? So soon? However, the bell stopped any further action, apart from that in Cooper's corner, where, as had happened in the Clay corner the previous break, his seconds worked overtime to staunch the blood. On balance, the second round was Cooper's, which put him two up. The pressure was clearly on Clay to 'do something'.

The third started with Cooper fresh from the attention of his seconds: the bleeding had been stopped, and thoughts banished of his vulnerable eyebrows. With the two men sparring and weaving, both quietly scoring off each other, after ninety seconds the round was evenly balanced. Suddenly, with a speed and ferocity which took the breath away, Clay erupted. A charge of venom appeared to flash through him, as two lightning, and immensely powerful, lefts to Cooper's face flung the Britisher's head back. It looked bad: soon Cooper staggered slightly around the ring, momentarily shaken by the comparatively unexpected fury of the American attack. Blood trickled down Cooper's cheek: this time the damage looked greater than before, but not unbearable. The crowd, sensing danger, raised the chant higher in volume and pitch: "COO-PER, COO-PER", but Clay knew he had done well. Within a minute of his attack he danced around Cooper, slapping his gloves together in eager anticipation. Cooper's defence held, and the bell brought blessed relief. Clay's round.

Cooper's new cut did not catch his seconds out: with the skill and speed of master-surgeons they worked quietly on the wound, and at the start of the fourth the blood had once again ceased to flow. Indeed, Clay was tempted to attack the wound: Cooper took three more jabs to the damaged skin but still the cut refused to open. Clay realised he had a lot of work to do, and again attacked Cooper's head, this time with success: the blood pressure broke through the flimsy surface tension and trickled down into Cooper's eye. He blinked involuntarily, and Clay, encouraged, attacked again. His prediction of a fifth-round win looked as though his Cassandra-like skills would once again be proved right. The crowd was incensed, and screamed at the spectacle, at the same time as Clay dropped his guard. A classic punch, Cooper's left hook was no mirage: perfectly timed, he caught Clay full-square with it. Clay recalled later, "suddenly something exploded against my jaw", and he fell back against the ropes and to the floor, flat on his back, with his head resting against the bottom ropes. The stadium erupted in pandemonium as the spectators realised here was a fight indeed, but no sooner had the noise began its tremendous crescendo than the bell rang: few heard it, least of all the referee, who counted to four before signalling the end of the round. The bell had actually sounded before he counted to two. Clay was on his feet again and in his corner, while the excitement of the fifty thousand spectators reached fever-pitch. "Saved by the bell", was the phrase on many lips, and Cooper's adrenalin must have pumped through his veins as he sat in his corner, eager to go.

In Clay's corner, however, strange things were discovered: his glove was damaged, with a busted seam and with the filling coming out. A replacement had to be got, which delayed the start of the fifth round. It is a moot point whether the extra time this afforded Clay materially affected the result, but the delay could only have also increased Cooper's expectations. This, we all felt, was to be the most important round we had yet witnessed.

Eventually, the bell sounded, and the unexpected happened again. All eyes were on Cooper perhaps to finish off what he had so brilliantly achieved in round four, but Clay stormed out of his corner, a different boxer from that which we had seen before. He knew Cooper was dangerous if allowed to get through: perhaps he had under-rated the British boxer's class and determination. This time there would be no argument. At a speed which literally took the breath away, unbelievable in a heavyweight, and certainly never witnessed before in a British ring at this level, Clay's left fist struck Cooper's face time and time again with tremendous force and ferocity. Within twenty seconds Cooper's face was a pitiful sight: the blood poured out of him, down his face, into each crack on his lined skin and dropped, like through a faulty tap, onto his body, trunks and the ring. His left eye, totally unable to withstand this hurricane-like fire, was opened up appallingly. The crowd, minutes before, had been shouting for Cooper to finish it: now they could not shout loud nor often enough for Mr Little to end the contest. Nothing could be done. After one minute, fifteen seconds of round five, mercy and humanity asserted themselves over the relentless attack.

So Clay had won, in the fifth, as he had predicted. But for many watching, Cooper's performance was hardly less impressive. Of the four completed rounds, Cooper had clearly won three, and had he been given more time in the fourth might well have caused a major upset. Clay knew the force of Cooper's punching, as well as being surely surprised by the Englishman's speed and resilience. But in the last analysis, it was not so much Clay's extra height, his extra reach or his extra weight. It was his speed, his dazzling, pulverising speed which enabled him to kill off, within twenty seconds of round five, any hopes British fight fans had for a serious contender to beat Cassius Clay.

(5)
February 25th 1964
v SONNY LISTON (USA) THE WORLD HEAVYWEIGHT CHAMPION
venue: Convention Hall, Miami Beach, Florida
Cassius Clay: 15st 0½lb (210½lbs)
Sonny Liston: 15st 8lbs (218lbs)
Referee: Barney Felix
Attendance: 8,297

Clay had been after Liston for a long time, then the holder of the richest prize in boxing: the heavyweight championship of the world. The night Clay beat Cooper in London he knew Liston was ready for him. Liston's manager, Jack Nilon, flew to London and made the offer in the winner's dressing-room. Apparently, Clay's incessant baiting of Liston in public had worked. Without going through many other contestants, Clay had laid himself on the line and literally talked his way to the contest. He almost talked himself out of it.

The great civil rights movement in the United States had scored a notable triumph the previous year with a massive demonstration in Washington. President Kennedy came from the White House and publicly joined with the movement. On November 22nd 1963, he was assassinated in Dallas, Texas, and this shocking crime not only symbolised the death of reasoned sympathy with those less fortunate than others, but also marked the rise of violence in political terms. For a generation, the Western World had generally been free from assassination and public violence, and the youth movement which Kennedy in a sense represented and also strove to embrace had not known the seething hatred which was typified by the Kennedy killing. At a stroke, the world learned an old truth: there is no answer to the bullet in the back of the head. The one man who might have done so much for the underdog was gone, and for lesser mortals rather more drastic solutions seemed the only way to achieve their aims. The Black Muslim movement in the United States, seeking to re-establish the pride in ethnic origin which had been submerged for so long, proclaimed a more self-assertive attitude and more dignity in being black than had ever happened before. Cassius Clay had known prejudice and insult all his life — as we saw earlier, even after he had returned to Louisville with his Olympic medal — and to those whites, unconvinced by Kennedy's liberalism, any move to enfranchise the blacks was to be resisted. It says a great deal for Clay's determination and belief in his rights to hold his own religious and political views that the threat of the promoter of the Liston-Clay fight, a man called MacDonald, to call off the match at a few hours' notice because of Clay's association with the Black Muslims was met by a stance of immutable clarity from Clay. He was willing to sacrifice the chance of winning the one thing he had sought for so long rather than compromise his own beliefs. Clay and his entourage had packed their bags and loaded them into their bus, ready to leave, before the fight was on again, at the eleventh hour.

The weigh-in was incredible. Apart from the public baiting, which included driving to Liston's home at 2.00am one morning and waking the neighbourhood with horns, shouting and general disturbance, Clay's behaviour at what is normally a straightforward preamble was startling. Kicking and screaming at the top of his voice, while his handlers tried to restrain him, Clay hurled abuse and jibes at Liston during the whole of the weigh-in procedure. He almost shouted himself hoarse, so much so that when Dr Robbins, the chief physician of the Miami Beach Boxing Commission, examined Clay after Liston had been examined, he declared Clay was "a man scared to death." "He is emotionally unbalanced", the doctor continued, with evidence for his diagnosis: Clay's pulse rate at the weigh-in was 120 (it had been 54 the week before) and Liston's was an average 80. However, the doctor declared Clay to be a superb athlete, but Clay's unprecedented behaviour caused him to fall foul of the Boxing Commission: they fined him $2,500 for misbehaviour at the weigh-in. That day, at the races held in Hialeah Park, Miami, the fourth race was won by an 8-1 outsider, named Cassius. The boxing press, however, were in no mood to back outsiders: out of almost fifty papers, forty-four predicted a win for Liston, and only three or four reckoned on Clay.

Mr MacDonald might well have wished the fight could have been called off. He had paid $625,000 for promotional rights for the fight, but only $402,000 was taken in attendance money. The fight seemed a foregone conclusion and many thought Liston was unbeatable, a mean machine of demonic destructive power. His hands were so huge and thick that special gloves had to be made to fit them. He was called a man without pity, ferocious and immensely strong, who had beaten just about every other heavyweight of any consequence. And Clay was the blabbermouth, the young self-aggrandising braggart who had won all his professional fights, but against men of lesser calibre than Liston had beaten. Or so it seemed: few wanted to turn out for a fight that seemed so predictable in its course.

But not all fight fans were as nonplussed as the Miami residents. As it happened, the Clay-Liston fight in 1964 created an all-time record both in attendance and money for closed-circuit coverage in the USA and Canada. Liston, in one of the few retorts drawn by Clay's baiting that "Liston will fall in eight because I am great", said Clay could have the championship if he stayed eight seconds in the ring with him, and the bookies had no doubts: Liston was favourite at 8-1 on. Consequently, when the bell signalled the start of the bout, the contrast between the two boxers was startling. Clay's previous fight, against Henry Cooper, showed he wasn't the only heavyweight with speed, but against Liston, he appeared a whirlwind, bobbing and weaving, ducking and backing away like a perfectly poised fencing master, his hit-and-run tactics disconcerting Liston and the crowd. No heavyweight, least of all a contender for the world crown, has a right to behave like this. Why doesn't he fight? Surely he can't keep this up? — these were the thoughts of the hardened observers. All the while, Clay was scoring with his deadly accurate left jabs, while Liston, when he caught Clay with his rare lefts, appeared lumbering, gorilla-like, by comparison. And then something extraordinary happened. Liston, whether from a combination of punches from the challenger or from one of his own left jabs, suddenly felt a dull crack in his shoulder. Almost as suddenly, it was forgotten in the speed of the moment, as the bell brought the first round to an end.

The champion kept the news of his shoulder to himself: round two started in much the same way as round one, with Clay again dancing, hopping around Liston, pushing, jabbing and knocking little by little the champion's face and body. Liston seemed strangely muted: where was the mean machine, the man without pity? No-one doubted his strength, but strength itself was of no consequence if the target against which it was to be used did not stay still long enough to be hit. In no other of Clay's title fights, prior to 1967, was the couplet 'float like a butterfly, sting like a bee', so clearly demonstrated. But no-one knew, apart from Liston, of the growing pain that surged through the champion's left shoulder.

Clay must have sensed, as he came out for the third, that he had a great chance. He did not know of Liston's injury, and could hardly understand why the champion was putting up such a comparatively subdued performance. But a subdued Liston was still Liston, and still a threat. Liston's left shoulder and arm might be hurting, but he could still manoeuvre well, and his right arm was still functioning. He had a lot of fight left in him, and then suddenly, like Clay did with Cooper in London eight months before, Clay literally cut loose in the third with a series of combination punches to Liston's head of dazzling speed. Clay's speed again caught everyone by surprise, but his strength, always suspect by those who thought they knew better, was also ferocious as he cut Liston's cheek, under the champion's left eye. For the first time in his life, Liston had been cut, and he felt his blood ooze down his face and splat on the floor. The round was Clay's and the champion was in trouble. During the break his seconds worked on the painful shoulder and his cut face, putting a caustic liniment solution on the damaged arm muscles. It seemed to work, for the fourth was more evenly matched than the previous round, but the shoulder could not stand up to much more of the jarring, searing pain which flooded through it every time Liston caught Clay, or Clay caught Liston. The champion's hope of getting relief from the pain was to engage Clay in clinches, and his shoulder, rubbed with the liniment, caught Clay's head. Some of the solution smeared onto Clay's forehead and ran down into Clay's eyes. Gradually, Clay could not see. His eyes stung, horribly, and he could only fend off the damaged champion.

During the break before the fifth, Clay protested vigorously to Angelo Dundee: "I can't see." The bell rang for the start of the fifth, and Clay still sat there, immobile, his eyes near-blinded from the liniment, now diluted by his own seconds' sponging and wiping his face. Dundee pushed him from the seat, and Clay staggered out into the fifth, to the unknowing onlooker like a drunken ballet-dancer. Clay again was reduced to fending-off tactics, and boxing was forgotten as both men tried to stay out of trouble. Liston's shoulder had again been saturated with the liniment, and seemed better, but only because of Clay's comparative inaction. Gradually, the trouble with Clay's eyes cleared in the fifth, but the trouble with Liston's shoulder naturally got worse. By the end of the fifth, Clay's eyes had returned to normal, and he finished the round with a fusillade of vicious jabbing left and right shots to Liston's head.

In the sixth it was all Clay: he knew he had Liston beat, though exactly why was irrelevant, and the contender kept up a punishing attack of sudden hit-and-run jabs, cuts and crosses, in pure combination, as though it was an exhibition of how to box scientifically without getting hurt. Those correspondents of the forty-odd newspapers who predicted a Liston walk-over could hardly believe their eyes as Liston, the mean machine, the man without pity, was attacked in a prestissimo war of attrition by Clay. The pain in Liston's shoulder was now unbearable, and as the bell brought blessed relief from the onslaught, he walked slowly to his corner. Clay danced to his, clearly sensing the moment he had dreamed about for a decade was near: if he kept this up, he would be the next champion.

The bell sounded the start of the seventh: Clay sprang up. Liston did not. He sat there, unable to continue, unable to withstand the appalling pain in his shoulder and arm, and unwilling to be cut to ribbons by more unremitting punishment from Clay. The referee, in a few seconds, grasped the situation: Angelo Dundee knew it, too, but Clay could hardly believe his eyes as, momentarily, he stared in disbelief at the sphinx-like Liston. Then all hell broke loose: the ring was suddenly crowded with people piling into it. Dundee and Bundini were first, and Clay jumped almost three feet into their arms, as they hugged each other in delirious delight. It was all over.

The punters stared in shocked amazement: representatives of the Miami Beach Boxing Commission could not understand what had

31

happened. How could Liston have given up so easily? What went wrong? Was it a fix? Why did he retire? All these questions could only be answered by a medical examination, and Dr Robbins, together with seven other doctors, examined Liston after the fight at St Francis Hospital, Miami. The Boxing Commission withheld Liston's purse, pending the examination. In the early hours of the following day, Dr Robbins read the report of the doctors:

> "It is our conclusion, after examination of Charles Liston, at St Francis Hospital, that he suffered injury to the biceps tendon connecting to the left shoulder with the result that there is a separation and tear of the muscle fibre and some haemorrhage into the muscle belly."

Because of Liston's serious and obvious injury, Dr Robbins recommended that his purse should be paid. Sonny Liston had been beaten, and, against all odds, Cassius Marcellus Clay, Jr, was the new Heavyweight Champion of the World.

During the celebration party, Cassius Clay was invited to become a full member of the Nation of Islam. At the press conference the following day, the new champion declared his faith. "I don't have to be what you want me to be. I am free to be what I want." Just what that was to cost the champion, few could foretell, but his decision cost him his name. The name he adopted, on becoming the most famous recruit to the Black Muslims, was first, Cassius X (his 'waiting' name) and then his 'original name', Muhammad Ali.

CHAPTER SIX

Champion for the First Time

(1)
May 25th 1965
v SONNY LISTON (USA)
venue: St Dominic's Arena, Lewiston, Maine
Muhammad Ali: 15st 0½lbs (210½lbs)
Sonny Liston: 15st 8lbs (218lbs)
Referee: Jersey Joe Walcott
Attendance: 2,434

In the fifteen months since his sensational win over Liston, Ali's increasing involvement with the more militant aspects of the civil rights movement and the Black Muslims made him a world charismatic figure. He had been invited to visit several African countries, where he was given VIP treatment, and a tremendous public welcome. Back home in the USA, Ali's publicity had little to do with his athleticism. Far removed from boxing, for the first time a black champion said he was proud to be black, to be champion on his own terms, and not on the terms on those who would somehow 'allow' him to be champion. Many right-wing reactionaries in the United States were incensed at Ali's success, his continuing insistence on his personal supremacy in the ring, and his right to choose whatever religion he saw fit. Many prominent people find their lives threatened from time to time, usually by deranged persons, but with the assassination of President Kennedy and the growing violence which erupted intermittently throughout America, the authorities were forced to take seriously threats to people as exposed, as frequently quoted, and as hated as Ali had become by a section of the population. He was the most talked-about boxer for decades: his exploits had won the interest of millions of people, and not only in America, who would not normally bother with boxing. Few people find arrogant boasters attractive, and many wanted to see Ali licked. Somehow, the Louisville Lip should be silenced, but the extremists thought that if a boxer could not do it, then a bullet could.

The rematch with Liston was postponed first because of a virus infection which laid Ali low a few days before the scheduled fight, but it had also become increasingly difficult, because of Ali's political associations, to find a city that would grant him a licence to fight. After much to-ing and fro-ing, the town of Lewiston in Maine was fixed for the venue, which accounts for the smallest attendance at a heavyweight title fight possibly of all time — certainly for many decades. As the time came for Ali's rematch with Liston, the threats against his life grew: policemen had to get up early to hide every five or six hundred feet of the route of Ali's regular early-morning run, in case a lone sniper was hidden. One morning, before the usual guard arrived, Ali's camp was actually attacked by a gang of gunmen, but this news was withheld until after the fight, in case more determined would-be assassins took it upon themselves to finish the job. Secret service personnel mingled with the attendees at Ali's training camp; his food and water were checked thoroughly: in short, the pressures on him were almost unbearable. Ali still had to train. It was his first title defence and he had gone out on a limb. Many thought Liston could whip him easily. In addition, Ali had other immense pressures. His religious conversion was widely disbelieved either as a publicity gimmick or as the action of a simpleton who had been used and duped by sinister and smarter people. Few realised that Ali was serious, and meant it. On June 4th 1964, Ali married but his wife, as he said "the first woman I ever loved", could not follow Ali's religious principles. She dropped this bombshell three days before the Liston rematch, the same day that Jimmy Ellis, an Ali sparring partner, caught the champion with a sharp right to the ribs that Ali thought could have been a fracture. Ali decided to keep the injury to himself, as, so soon before the fight, the contest would almost certainly have had to be postponed a second time.

Another curious episode arose from the first fight: it transpired that Ali's Louisville group of sponsors, headed by Bill Faversham, had signed a contract with a firm called Inter-Continental Promotions, Inc (in which Liston owned $47\frac{1}{2}$ % of the shares) giving them promotional rights to Ali's next fight. In other words, whether Ali had won the championship or not in February 1964, Sonny Liston had, prior to that bout taking place, bought a substantial share of the right to promote Ali's next fight. A strange move, and one which aroused the interest and anger of many boxing people.

Apart from these problems, which any athlete could well have done without, the boxing experts were having a field day. Ali was champion, no doubt about it, but could he punch? He was fast, tall, strong, self-confident, but the Cooper fight had shown his vulnerability. If Ali was to remain world champion, he would have to demonstrate he could punch as hard and as mean as any other boxer on the planet. Ali's success the previous year had confounded nearly all the critics: a dangerous fact, for no 'expert' likes to be proved wrong, and those that are almost invariably bear grudges to the extent that they never miss an opportunity to put down the person who has exposed their own incompetence.

A lot was on Ali's mind, and shoulders, as he stepped into the ring in Lewiston, Maine, that night. Liston, too, had much to avenge: Ali was the first fighter to cut him, the first to draw blood, and maybe the shoulder injury the previous year was just an unlucky freak of circumstance. Liston, in normal conditions, would have been anxious to demonstrate his superiority over Ali. But the conditions were not normal: it was public knowledge that threats to Ali's life were being taken seriously by the FBI, who with J. Edgar Hoover at the top, might have looked somewhat askance at the situation. There Ali would be a moving target, in blinding lights, easy pickings for a sniper: and who would be in the ring with him? Charles 'Sonny' Liston himself, innocent of Black Power Politics, unconcerned with civil rights or religious differences. All it needed was a Ku Klux Klan fanatic from the South to travel north to Maine to put an end to both black fighters in full view of the whole world.

Whatever imaginings might have gone through either fighter's mind before the bout were dispelled by the clarity of the bell: Liston, it was soon obvious, was deadly serious, and had learned much from their first meeting. Ali began as before, dancing, weaving, bobbing, tantalising the slower Liston, who, this time, instead of being bemused by the speed of Ali, attempted to match him. He chased Ali, followed him around the ring, but it was clear he would have just as hard a time to hit him as he had before. Liston swung several times at Ali, punches which would have shaken a slower man had they connected, but Ali circled him, evading them with disdain, in a continuous anti-clockwise motion, forcing Liston forever to move to his right. Quite simply, Liston could not get a fix on Ali, who increased his circling speed, occasionally slowing to catch the disoriented Liston on the jaw. After a minute of this strange boxing, Ali caught Liston with a powerful right to the jaw, and then another right, for all the world seeming to lack the power of the first, followed by a left hook. The left hook missed, for by this time Liston was on the way to the floor. In the previous fight, Liston had been cut by Ali for the first time in his career, and now, in the first round he had been knocked down by Ali, for the first time in his career. Liston was on his back. Ali stood over him, shouting at him to get up, and Jersey Joe Walcott, with some difficulty, forced Ali to a neutral corner for the count. Once the referee's attention was back with Liston, he did not know how far the count had gone, and sought the help of the timekeeper, Mr McDonough. The uproar from the two and a half thousand spectators in the smallish auditorium was so tremendous that no-one could hear anything through the wall of sound. Liston struggled to one knee but fell on his back again. Then he rose to his feet and Ali, eager to home in on his foe, was after him. The fight might have continued had not Jersey Joe realised that Liston, had, in fact, been counted out by the timekeeper. It was all over, the fastest world heavyweight championship fight in almost sixty years. Including the count, the film of the fight lasts one minute, fifty-two seconds.

If uproar greeted Ali's first win over Liston, then the English language has to be searched for words to describe the reaction to this second win. An infernal noise, from the tumultuous, screaming crowd was witness to what had happened. The Black Muslim, the boasting, bombastic, loud-mouthed Muhammad Ali had done it again. But this time, few believed what they had seen. Where was the man of iron, this neolithic fighting-machine called Liston? Knocked senseless in a hundred seconds by a punch which appeared to land with the ferocity, as one observer wrote, of a cream puff.

The critics, the experts, the writers raced to be the first with the words to condemn what they had seen. Mc MacKenzie, President of the World Boxing Association, watching the fight in Toronto, said the contest was "unfitting, unkempt, illegal and a disgrace to boxing". However, the WBA could hardly be dispassionate over the fight, as they had been involved (through Mr MacKenzie's predecessor, one Ed Lassman) in a shabby move to strip Ali of his title, and refused to recognise the rematch.

But whatever anyone said, the result stood: Ali had won an unbelieve-able, staggering victory. The film of the fight does not really answer all the questions that remained, for a punch which can cause damage or momentary loss of control, or sheer blinding pain, need not necessarily be seen to have force. Watching the fight again, Ali's right to the jaw, just before the blow which seemed to floor Liston, could well have been the one which did the most damage. It was a real punch, unexpected, on a man who had been disoriented by Ali's dancing tactics for almost a minute. It must have hurt, and probably caught Liston at a fractionally sensitive spot in his central nervous system. A few seconds later, in spite of Liston's strength and stamina, the next punch was the one, landing in about the same place, fast and twisting, which lifted Liston's left foot (a picture publised in *Time* magazine clearly shows the raised feet of Liston before he fell) and literally pushed Liston over: dazed by the first, not having time to recover, the second jab was the *coup de grâce*.

Only one thing is permanent and unchangeable: that which has actually happened. Nothing can alter events of the past, and Ali had sensationally defended his title. Now they all wanted to challenge him, and his next six title defences occurred within twelve months.

(2)
November 22nd 1965
v FLOYD PATTERSON (USA)
venue: Rotunda, Las Vegas Convention Center
Muhammad Ali: 15st 0lbs (210lbs)
Floyd Patterson: 14st 0¾lbs (196¾lbs)
Referee: H Kruse
Attendance: 7,402

Ali's second, astonishing win over Liston further incensed his
detractors — of whom there were many — and made the contenders for
the heavyweight crown eager to have a crack at toppling the young
champion. Ali's meteoric rise, his flamboyant manner, his connexions
with the Black Muslims and his growing trouble with the Army (which
was soon to become his most pressing problem) had raised several
question-marks over him, but they were largely unconnected with the
man's ability as a boxer. Many people wanted to see him beaten just
because he was Muhammad Ali (although still known to the public at
large as Cassius Clay), and for no other reason. Surely, one might
reasonably have thought, there was a challenger who could give this
Louisville Lip his comeuppance? But who was there? Ali had sensationally beaten the previous champion twice, but there were still many
people who felt that both wins had been flukes — if nothing more.
What about the man Liston beat for the title — Floyd Patterson? He
had been champion *twice* before, regaining the title from Ingemar
Johansson of Sweden in 1961. Eighteen months later, Patterson was
knocked out in the first round by Liston in Chicago. Furthermore,
unlike Ali's three previous fights, Patterson was much closer to the
champion in age. Indeed, Patterson had been the youngest man ever to
hold the title, when he won it two months before his twenty-second
birthday. Ali, when he first beat Liston, was twenty-two years, one
month. Patterson also possessed a proven knockout punch, as Cooper
did, but perhaps rather more so, so it appeared the bout would be more
of a fight than Ali's outings with Liston.
  In the event, the crowd was disappointed: but the reason was not the
lack of ability on the part of either boxer, nor the failure of Ali to engage
his opponent. The root cause, and one which boxing enthusiasts had
still not generally grasped as fully as they might, was that Ali's style of
fighting was so totally original, so utterly unlike anything else that had
ever been seen in a heavyweight ring, that no living boxer could be
found to match him on his own terms. Ali's legendary speed and lightning footwork made his early opponents appear like Frankenstein
monsters in comparison. Nor is this a criticism of other heavyweights:
men who weigh around two hundred pounds (fourteen to fifteen stone)
or more are not usually noted for their grace and athleticism. Ali's

uncanny ability to move with the lithe agility of a flyweight set him apart. The butterfly first had to be caught if he was to be transfixed.

It was Ali's opponent who made the early running — or, rather, attempted to. As with Cooper and with Liston's second bout, Patterson came out eager for the fray, and in spite of Ali's dancing and persistent jabbing, Patterson managed to catch the champion with a number of hefty body blows, including one particularly solid punch which seemed to fractionally halt the fast-moving Ali. But again it was the speed of Ali which proved his most effective defence. There can be nothing more frustrating for a boxer, especially a heavyweight (and perhaps even more so for a twice world champion) to fling powerful punches at empty air. It is a waste of energy, and a continuous fruitless policy that gradually saps the strength and angers the mind. Patterson, even in the first round, which was his best and probably won by him on points, was already being subjected to Ali's telling combination of swift jabs and dancing feet.

In round two, Patterson saw the futility of fighting as he had done in the first, in spite of one or two successes. The physical fact of Ali's eight inches superior reach over Patterson was daunting: Patterson himself tried jabbing Ali, trying to engage him in clinches with a chance of wearing him down, of pinning the butterfly still for a fraction of a second, in the hope that on the break he could catch Ali with his attention momentarily distracted, as Cooper had done. There was a danger in this ploy. Patterson, for all his great skill and superb ring-craft, possessed what had been called — a little unkindly, perhaps — a 'glass chin'. If Ali could catch the challenger with the kind of punch that floored Liston, then it would be curtains for Patterson. Therefore Patterson had much to do. He had to engage Ali at close quarters and protect his own chin at the same time. This required split-second timing and almost an instinctive approach to boxing. Luckily, Patterson was young enough for these qualities to be unimpaired.

For all this, Patterson's change of tactics were of little use. Ali's reach — his second line of defence after his footwork — was of such literally over-riding consequence that Patterson could do little more than find himself at the end of Ali's incessant jabbing. However, maybe Patterson's tactics would work eventually. If he could absorb Ali's left arm jabs, and still find a way through to engage the champion, then he would be in with a considerable chance. Ali knew this, too.

In the third, Ali came out as though it were the beginning of a three-round exhibition match. Suddenly, as though he knew what Patterson's tactics were, and had realised the only route open to the challenger, Ali's speed and footwork were positively mercurial. Flashing, dancing, dazzling, fleet of foot and of punch, Ali harried, worried, and landed volley after volley of consecutive lefts and combination punches to Patterson's head and body. It was almost unbelievable: surely this could not be a bout for the heavyweight championship of the world? Patterson appeared immobile, static, totally unable to cope with the whirlwind which was charging around him. From this moment on, no matter how long the fight was to last, it was crystal clear to everyone that Ali would not be beaten by Floyd Patterson.

Ali himself must have sensed this, for he came charging out at the start of the fourth with a "this is it!" shout to Patterson. This gladiatorial challenge roused Patterson, who struck first, with a blur of punches to Ali, several of which struck their target. For the first time in the fight, the crowd saw the possibility that it might, after all, develop into a contest. But Ali absorbed Patterson's punches easily, and we saw another side to the champion. His speed and his reach meant that few boxers had ever got close to him. What was glimpsed in this round, however fleetingly, was Ali's capacity to withstand heavy combination punches. Ali's speed proved another asset to him, in a slightly different manner. In the fourth, unable to finish off Patterson (though to be fair, it would have appeared a herculean task), Ali was occasionally caught by the former champion on the ropes. The speed and reflexes he showed on such occasions were, again, little short of amazing. He slid off the ropes easily, fluently, almost magically, when any kind of danger appeared from Patterson. In seconds, Ali turned the tables on the challenger and proceeded to score again with a flurry of jabbing lefts to Patterson's head.

The fifth round marked time for both men. In the fourth, Ali had taken a little more punishment than he anticipated at the end of the third, rather more so than he had taken professionally in over two years (since fighting Cooper). Now was the time, when he was clearly ahead on points, not to get himself in the kind of situation which would enable Patterson to dictate the fight. If Ali was to remain champion, and few could really believe that he could not so remain, then Patterson must be defused, and it did not mean going for a knockout. In the fifth, therefore, Ali contented himself with a more relaxed round, testing the pulse of his opponent by letting the fight tick over gently, although occasionally flashing the accurate left jabs. In this round, Patterson later felt the first twinge from an old back injury, which naturally contributed to his muted performance.

The sixth found Ali utterly in control: the previous round, lacking high drama, had in fact been used intelligently by the champion. Now in the sixth Ali carefully picked his moment and attacked suddenly, with a demonic ferocity reminiscent of the fifth round with Cooper. A deadly right landed to Patterson's head, and was immediately followed by three staccato lefts also to the head. Too much for any man to take, Patterson staggered and fell to his knees, taking a supplicatory count of eight before rising to continue. The end was near, it seemed, not only of the round, but of the fight.

The seventh saw Ali again on the attack, but Patterson defended strongly, resisting all the champion's efforts to get through his tight and almost desperate defence. Again and again, however, Ali scored, dancing and skipping the while. The eighth was similar, and so was the ninth, with Patterson becoming more and more unable to answer Ali. In many ways, had this not been a fight for the world crown, the referee should have stopped the contest in the ninth or tenth rounds, for Patterson became badly battered by the unremitting accuracy of Ali's deadliest punches. If Ali had not been so fast, in fact if he had stopped prancing around the ring for a few moments and laid into Patterson, he could have felled the challenger at will, but his speed almost became a hindrance as his energy carried him along in top gear.

The tenth and eleventh rounds continued the story: Patterson was surely worn down, erased from contention, almost destroyed before the Nevada crowd. Any doubts as to Ali's stamina were dispelled by this fight, and finally, in the twelfth round, after two minutes, eighteen seconds, the referee finally called the contest off. Patterson, twice knocked out in the first rounds of previous fights, had withstood — with ever-decreasing effectiveness — the relentless Ali, and some felt Ali's previous Liston win, within two minutes of the first round, was even more dubious compared with his inability to put Patterson away. Although the view was widely expressed at the time, subsequent fights have shown that this match with Patterson was a demonstration of another of Ali's natural skills: his stamina, his manner of fighting each bout in a different way. Although his technique in these early world title fights remained basically the same, his approach, his extraordinary manner of fighting a psychological battle with his opponents in the ring as well as a physical one, varied with each opponent. This is not to say that Ali was so far beyond defeat at this time from anyone (for he himself knew that the contenders were not all push-overs) but to demonstrate Ali's uncanny knack of doing the unexpected in such a way that, upon reflection, it appeared to be the inevitable thing to do. Whether Ali really hated Liston is irrelevant: he certainly knew he could beat him, and beat him well. And so he *had* to do that — he had to demonstrate his prowess in public. With Patterson, twice world champion, another approach was needed. A sudden knock-out, and the rumours might well have been flying again in another way. But a public showing of his capability to wage a war of attrition, so menacing and pitiless in its construction, proved he was able to fight a long fight on quite different lines. Writers at the time were not convinced as to Ali's suitability to be champion, but the most telling facts at the end of the bout are the photographs of the champion and the beaten challenger — Ali is unmarked, as 'pretty' as ever: Patterson is a tragic figure, his left eye shut fast, puffed and obscene, his face awash with blood. That damage was not caused by a man who could not punch. But it could have been helped by someone who was not fit enough to defend himself, as Patterson later claimed concerning the return of his back injury. In the ring, however, there are no excuses. Ali won, fair and square.

(3)
March 29th 1966
v GEORGE CHUVALO (CANADA)
venue: The Maple Leaf Gardens, Toronto, Canada
Muhammad Ali: 15st 4½lbs (214½lbs)
George Chuvalo: 15st 6lbs (216lbs)
Referee: Jackie Silvers
Attendance: 14,000

George Chuvalo, the Canadian heavyweight champion, was born in
Toronto and learned his fighting at first on the streets of that city, and
graduated, via the local gyms, to become the most formidable boxer
Canada had produced for many years. He possessed immense strength,
and was fractionally heavier than Ali when they met. However,
compared with Ali, Chuvalo's appearance lacked the superbly-
proportioned body of the champion. Chuvalo looked like an old-time
heavyweight, powerful, ragged, with muscles bulging from his thick-set
body.

The fight was in many ways the most interesting Ali had fought since
winning the championship. Although not strictly speaking a title fight
it was Ali's first fight against a white boxer, also his first in a foreign
country since beating Liston, and, as it turned out, the first for over
three years where his opponent forced Ali to go the distance. Chuvalo
refused to go down.

Indeed, the fight began with powerhouse action from Chuvalo. He
went after Ali, staggering, barging his way through the by-now famous
left jabs and immense reach. Close to Ali, crowding him in the corners,
Chuvalo let fly a series of hefty blows low to the body. Had Chuvalo not
been a local boy, the referee would doubtless have warned him, for
several of these punches were very low, quite clearly fouls. Ali, however, by this time an experienced man at taking unmerited punishment
outside the ring, appeared almost to laugh at Chuvalo's tactics. It could
have proved a disastrous reaction by the champion, for Chuvalo
continued this approach throughout the next three rounds. In fact, in
the first four rounds of this fight Ali absorbed a greater amount of
punishment from Chuvalo than he had possibly taken in all his
previous title defences put together. It is a measure of his capacity and
resilience that he emerged unscathed from this onslaught. It is also
curious to ponder why Ali did not use his famous speed to back away
from Chuvalo's lunges. It almost seems as though Ali was deliberately
inviting Chuvalo to hit him with all he had, fouling in the process if
need be, just to show that here was another aspect of Ali which had not
been seen in public before.

At one point, to the amazement of the crowd, and probably to
Chuvalo's disbelief, Ali stood still, with his arms raised high, openly
challenging the Canadian to hit him. It seemed a crazy thing to do (and

41

should not be adopted by aspiring fighters) but on reflection it was the most humiliating thing one boxer could do to another. Without hitting Chuvalo, Ali showed his public contempt for a boxer, however worthy, however strong, who was, in the last analysis, not in the same class as the champion. Ali's contemptuous nickname for Chuvalo, 'The Washerwoman' (because Chuvalo had a habit of letting fly with both arms in a gesticulating manner), was changed to 'The Washerman' — possibly an element of faint praise from Ali. By daring Chuvalo to hit him, Ali followed that by closing in, around the Canadian, with the certainty of a hound who has the fox at bay. Little by little, as before, Ali began to pick off Chuvalo, with an accuracy that still has to be seen to be believed. Gradually, round after round, Chuvalo was reduced in stature by a fighting machine which was totally in command of the bout. Ali's left jabs, again and again, like lightning flashes, coiled across space into Chuvalo's face, never missing, almost invariably homing in on the target as if directed by radar. As before with Patterson, no man could match this. Soon, Chuvalo's face lost it shape and colour, as blotches and then blood appeared, changing his appearance. Chuvalo was not champion of Canada for nothing, however: heavier than Patterson, he had more to absorb. It says much for Chuvalo's strength of character that he stood up, literally, to Ali's formidable repertoire. Ali unleashed everything against Chuvalo: his incessant jabs, some flying hooks, and a couple of immense bolos, but Chuvalo took the lot. In taking it, he was disfigured, but he found the strength to continue attacking Ali in the only way he could. Like a British Infantryman advancing at the first Battle of the Somme in the teeth of withering fire, Chuvalo's dogged persistence brought the crowd to its feet on several occasions. Late in the bout, from the twelfth round onwards, Chuvalo gamely struggled to find strength for a knockout blow: a points win was never on. If only he could keep going, and maybe wear Ali down, then, and then . . . But it was all ifs and buts and maybes. Ali had never before come across a fighter quite like Chuvalo. The Canadian appeared to have an inexhaustible capacity for absorbing everything that was thrown at him, but in return he never had the punching ability to fight back, as he knew he must. Even in the fifteenth, the farthest point any boxer had taken Ali, Chuvalo came on again and again, like a tank, but Ali, although beginning to tire visibly from his constant movement, still continued to score. At one point in the final round, it seemed as though Chuvalo might do it, as his persistence paid off: he got through to Ali, and caught him with a right to the champion's chin, a punch which still contained some power, as Ali appeared momentarily shaken by it. It is impossible to know if he was shaken as much by the force of the punch itself as by the tiredness even he was feeling towards the end.

And so the fight ended, with Ali having been taken the full fifteen rounds for the first time ever, and it showed a new side to him. There had never been any real doubt that he could go the distance, but as no-one had ever seen him do it before, it was virgin territory. Chuvalo, apart from his opening punches, had hurt Ali on several occasions, and the bout, although one-sided, became a real fight with Ali having to work to score and to win. He did, unanimously, and in the process inflicted deep punishment on Chuvalo, whose face at the end was likened to a tomato. Both eyes were badly cut, but Chuvalo's own personal boast had been kept: he had never been knocked out in his life, and not even Muhammad Ali could do that.

(4)
May 21st 1966
v HENRY COOPER (GREAT BRITAIN)
venue: Arsenal Football Club Stadium, Highbury, North London
Muhammad Ali: 15st 1½lbs (211½lbs)
Henry Cooper: 13st 6lbs (188lbs)
Referee: George Smith
Attendance: 41,000

Although Henry Cooper had fought Ali before, in 1963, that was of course before Ali became world heavyweight champion. For many people Cooper's knock-down of Ali in that fight had been one of the biggest upsets in the American's career, and Cooper's left hook was still of legendary and formidable proportions. He naturally wanted another crack at Ali, and within hours of the first defeat of Sonny Liston, Cooper challenged Ali to a world title fight. Over two years had passed since Ali became world champion, and in that time Cooper's age had increased to thirty-two. This was to tell against him statistically, but Cooper had been a consistent fighter and was always in the world ratings within a few points of Chuvalo, so, together with the substantial financial inducement, the prospect seemed exciting.

In a country which knew nothing first-hand about segregation, Black Muslims or Vietnam, Ali had become a popular hero in England. For that matter, Henry Cooper had raised his own popularity in England by his earlier fight with Ali, and many Englishmen boasted of that left hook. If only Henry could connect again. In challenging Ali for the title, Cooper became only the seventh British boxer to fight for the world heavyweight crown: all had been unsuccessful, and the two previous contenders, Don Cockell in 1955 against Rocky Marciano, and Brian London in 1959 against Floyd Patterson, had both been stopped within the distance.

Before the fight began, a request from Ali for a twenty-foot square ring (the maximum size permitted in international rules) was complied with. Some people believed it was the ropes which saved Ali in his previous fight with Cooper by breaking his fall, and preventing him from going completely flat on his back. Ali took a calculated risk by having a large ring. If he were to be caught again, it was less likely the ropes would assist him, and any in-fighting (where Ali could marginally be at a disadvantage) would not be so quickly brought to a halt by going for the ropes. However, Ali's fights with Patterson and Chuvalo had not always enabled him to dance away from danger. He probably felt the greater space the large ring afforded him would help in this respect. As before, Ali weighed in heavier than Cooper. It was an ominous sign, but it was a Saturday night in north London, and a good summer had come early to England. Sports fans were anticipating the World Cup, to be held in England that summer, so the Ali-Cooper fight marked a superb beginning to a memorable few months of sport.

Cooper's tactics in their first meeting had been sound, and he began round one of their second fight in similar fashion. It soon became apparent, however, that Ali's insistence on a larger ring worked very much in his favour. His speed was again the talk of the crowd. Cooper, throwing several murderous left hooks, landed them on thin air as Ali danced away. Cooper continued chasing Ali but the differences of age, height, weight and reach appeared insuperable barriers. It was not all one-sided: in rounds two and three Cooper fought back and landed several combination punches to Ali's head, clearly hurting him (as Ali later confirmed), and scoring well. Ali, however, again appeared the superior fighter, the greater tactician. Cooper's eyebrows were the prime target, those dangerously thin and too-prominent parts of his skull which had caused him so much trouble in the past. In the fourth, Cooper again came forward, calmly, totally unafraid of Ali's reputation and ability, but, during a close encounter in the closing minutes of the round, Ali suddenly flicked, like a deadly cobra, two incredibly fast — if not vehemently strong — left jabs to the face, landing in that deadly area around the eyes. Amazingly, no blood appeared, and in the fifth Cooper again came at Ali, whether through his own determination or whether, spider-like, at Ali's connivance. For no sooner was he at close quarters with the champion than Ali again unleashed his lightning strokes. Still no blood, and the crowd, sensing the Londoner had a good chance if he could again land the left hook, urged him on. A measure of Cooper's popularity can be gauged from the fact that in their first meeting, the syllables the crowd chanted were "COO-PER, COO-PER", but on this occasion it was the more intimate "'EN-RY, 'EN-RY." Some, however, could tell little difference between the last name and "A-LI, A-LI." Cooper more than survived the fifth, so he had at least travelled further with Ali than he had at their first meeting, but at the beginning of the sixth the crowd saw Ali at his most ferocious. A fast left and right to Cooper's head sent him back, momentarily disconcerted, and then Ali was in on his man, exchanging blows with Cooper at high speed. An early clinch and then the punches showed the return of the old killer: Cooper's left eye was invisible behind a flow of blood of sickening proportions. It gushed onto his body, shoulders and chest, absolutely unstoppable, except by surgery. Ali stepped back, almost aghast as Mr

Smith looked at the wound, and then signalled for the fight to continue. As Ali recalled: "I told the ref: 'You should stop it.' He looked at it and let him go on. He was wrong. I ran, only defending myself, hoping the ref would stop it. I had to throw a few punches but I did not aim for the cut because I knew the fight was over." In those seconds, all Cooper could hope for was a sudden knockout left to Ali's jaw, but the blood blinded him, and only his training, experience and instinct permitted him to lunge forward at the champion, who was by that time unwilling to inflict any more damage on Cooper's eye.

The fight was over, but Ali's statement was no sympathy-grabbing comment, the kind that some boxers make to justify their own behaviour. It was the plain truth. Cooper was taken to the casualty department of Guy's Hospital, in south London several miles away, where twelve stitches were inserted in the wound. Ali visited Cooper on his own, before he was taken to hospital, and the two men, who since their earlier meeting had possibly the most friendly rapport, parted on good terms. It was a sad night for British hopes, but the fight was clean, unmarred by unpleasantness, animosity, cries of "fake" or anything else, other than the way in which it had to end. On that night, true sportsmanship won, although Cooper at first thought his head had been cut in a clash at close quarters. The film of the fight does not support this, but merely confirms that Mr Smith ought really to have stopped the bout some forty-five seconds earlier.

(5)
August 6th 1966
v BRIAN LONDON (GREAT BRITAIN)
venue: Earl's Court Stadium, London
Muhammad Ali: 14st 13½lbs (209½lbs)
Brian London: 14st 5lbs (201lbs)
Referee: Harry Gibbs
Attendance: 11,000

Since Ali's first visit to London in 1963 he had taken to the English very much. Ali maintained that it was in England that he first felt treated like a human being from people in all walks of life. His defeats of Cooper, far from alienating the British, had actually endeared him to them, for his essentially extrovert personality had come like a breath of fresh air to a sport which, as far as most British citizens were concerned, was singularly lacking in mass appeal. In England, Ali was treated as a boxer first and foremost and not as a dangerous revolutionary about to overthrow the government, organised religion and corrupt the youth of the country. At that time, perhaps more than in any other part of the world, Muhammad Ali could feel relaxed and at home.

Less than two months after his devastating win over Henry Cooper, Ali was back in the British Isles for another title defence against the

British boxer Brian London. Whereas no-one would have criticised Henry Cooper for being an unworthy challenger, in Brian London a number of doubts had been raised as to his suitability. He hardly ranked in the world top ten ratings, and, although he had once before fought for the heavyweight championship of the world against Floyd Patterson, that had been seven years before, when he was pulverised in the eleventh. On the three occasions he had fought Henry Cooper, he had been beaten. Like Cooper, London was thirty-two and had had a similar fight record. He had lost 13 of his 48 professional bouts (Cooper 12 of 47), but few people gave him anything like the same chance Cooper had against Ali. But then, few had given Ali much of a chance against Liston in 1964 and, in the fight game, anything could happen.

The crowd, however, had no illusions: the vast Earl's Court Stadium was only half full, and within seconds of the opening bell, Ali realised he had a strange fight on his hands — or rather he did not have. London, no matter what faults he possessed, could never have been described as a worried fighter. Previously, he had gone into the ring with a fair amount of confidence but from the start of his fight with Ali he appeared tense and uncertain, even overawed by his opponent. Ali had always begun his fights in a certain manner: he would dance, letting his opponent make the first move, jabbing, running, scoring, sizing the man up the while. But with London, apart from the dancing and the scoring with the jabs, he had nothing to judge him on. London hardly aimed a blow at Ali in the first round, pushing rather than punching, and acting defensively, even though Ali did little purely attacking boxing, being merely content to pick off points from London's head with the famous left jab. One, possibly two, punches from London landed on Ali, but they appeared to have little force. The second round was a carbon copy, and the crowd began to shout their derision at the British boxer, who was unable to break out of the apprehension which had enveloped him since the start of the fight. There is no knowing what went through Ali's mind as he contemplated his opponent on this occasion, but at the start of the third, he sized up the inviting target, London's poorly defended large chin. Ali moved in, in the second minute of the third, pinning London into a corner. Ali let fly with fast, powerful punches, beginning with a vicious right cross, and two combinations struck firm at London's chin. It was Ali's first attack in the fight: it was also his last. London crumpled into a heap, and was counted out, barely moving, apart from a dim flicker of life as he raised his head a few inches from the canvas at about seven or eight.

Ali's fight with London was surely the easiest and most superfluous of his entire career. Although it was not the fastest (the second Liston fight had been that), in a sense it was, for London had crumpled and been beaten hollow at Ali's first attack. If that had happened in the first thirty seconds of the bout, then the fight might have entered the record-books as the fastest world championship knockout of all time.

46

(6)
September 10th 1966
v KARL MILDENBERGER (WEST GERMANY)
venue: Frankfurt, West Germany
Muhammad Ali: 14st 8lbs (204lbs)
Karl Mildenberger: 13st 12½lbs (194½lbs)
Referee: Teddy Waltham
Attendance: 45,000

While internal fractures in the boxing associations of the USA, and the growing public disquiet at Ali's avowed intention not to accept induction into the armed services when his draft came made it difficult for Ali to fight all comers in his own country, his trips to Canada and England for his last three bouts had opened up new possibilities: if he was prevented from fighting in the States, he would fight abroad. The extent to which this developed did not become apparent until almost ten years later, when, coupled with Ali's championship of black pride, title fights were held in countries which had never before witnessed such events. In the mid-1960s, Europe seemed to offer a viable alternative — at least in venues — to the USA. In addition, the European interest in Ali was totally unencumbered by the worrying nature of Ali's growing personal and political troubles at home.

It made sense, therefore, as well as money, to take on the European challengers on their own grounds and the fight against Mildenberger was, in many ways, a surprising and courageous choice. Mildenberger was a worthy challenger, unlike the performance put up by (or rather not put up by) Brian London, but a world championship heavyweight bout had not been fought in Germany for decades. Hardly any German boxers appeared in London after the second world war, so few Europeans knew much about Mildenberger. Consequently, Ali went into the ring against a man who was, in many ways, an unknown quantity. Mildenberger was Ali's fourth consecutive white opponent, and on the Saturday evening in September, the two men climbed into the ring for a fascinating and historic contest.

Mildenberger began with a quite remarkable advantage: he was a southpaw, the first Ali had fought for many years, and the first such challenger for the Ali crown. Ali in return appeared faintly uneasy against Mildenberger, but whether this was from the stance of the German or from his accelerating number of fights is uncertain. Because of Mildenberger's unfamiliar attack, Ali's usual dancing and jabbing had little effect on the German, who managed to get through Ali's defences with some ease, landing a number of fine scoring punches to Ali's head and body. It was good stuff: it began to appear as though the fight could develop into a real contest, even in the first round. Mildenberger was clearly totally unafraid of Ali, and came on against the champion in the second, continuing his solid build-up and attacking

47

style. Ali, by comparison, tended to back-pedal. Some people have put this reaction by Ali down to a certain disinterest, but it appeared that, as before with Chuvalo, and with London, Ali was using the opening rounds to size the man up on his own terms. Ali was quite able to take any punishment Mildenberger could dish out in the early rounds (as long as he stayed clear of real trouble) in order to see what the German was capable of. It was a remarkable way to fight a championship bout: Ali appeared unconcerned as to his own fate early on, confident and totally in command of his own ability. Still Mildenberger attacked throughout the second and most of the third, with punches that seemed to hurt Ali, especially low to the body. In the third, Ali later admitted that a powerful right cross from himself had damaged his hand as it landed on Mildenberger's face, but it was possible that punch which was the signal for Ali to begin to take command of the fight.

In the fourth, Ali, still nursing his damaged hand, opened up against the German's face. The by-now familiar attack of speed and precision, together with Ali's dancing, tantalising feet, dazzled his opponent. As before with Cooper and Liston, Chuvalo and Patterson, Ali's fury opened up the challenger's face, and a cut appeared under Mildenberger's right eye. Had he not been a southpaw, it would have been the left side of his face to be damaged, as had happened with Ali's orthodox opponents. The tide appeared almost inexorably to turn in Ali's favour, and as the fifth round began the patched-up Mildenberger seemed to be going the way of all flesh. Ali continued with unremitting accuracy, a volley of punches to the German, who finally succumbed in the last minute of the round: he hit the canvas, but got up and continued against the champion.

The crowd, too, was raised to its feet by Mildenberger's determination. Like Chuvalo before him, he refused to be put away (although it is possible Ali's damaged hand contributed to a lack of power from the champion), and Ali sent him to the canvas twice more. Both times Mildenberger got up and carried on. This was the first time in a championship bout Ali had witnessed such spirit, but in turn he continued his fearsome attack to Mildenberger's face. The German's eyes were red and swollen, but in the ninth round he found amazing reserves of energy as, getting his second wind, he hit out at Ali, with absolutely nothing to lose. The crowd could hardly believe it, and the excitement and tingling anticipation was electrifying, as, in terms of courage and sheer doggedness, Mildenberger took the round on points. This was Mildenberger's last fling. In the tenth and eleventh rounds Ali, with icy clarity, returned to the attack, and hit an uncountable number of times with skilful combination punches. Still the German refused to go down, but it was by now clear that he had no chance against the champion. In the second minute of the twelfth round, the referee could not permit the attack to continue: he pulled the champion off Mildenberger, and sent the challenger to the safety of his seconds.

After the fight, Ali admitted it was by far the most difficult of his three title defences in Europe, and it is fascinating, if futile, to speculate on what the outcome might have been had the fights taken place in reverse order. The result, however, was clear: in Europe the undisputed heavyweight champion of the world was Muhammad Ali. Pictures of Ali after the Mildenberger fight have to be seen to be believed: in less than four months he had successfully defended his world title three times in Europe, winning each bout within the distance, and yet his face was totally unmarked.

(7)
November 14th 1966
v CLEVELAND WILLIAMS (USA)
venue: Astrodome, Houston, Texas
Muhammad Ali: 15st 2¾lbs (212¾lbs)
Cleveland Williams: 15st 0½lb (210½lbs)
Referee: Harry Kessler
Attendance: 35,460

Ali returned to the United States having disposed of the notable European fighters, to face a succession of American challengers. His one slight physical problem, the damaged right hand sustained in the Mildenberger fight had cleared up, leaving him with purely personal problems. Although the cognoscenti of boxing had seen Ali's impressive European wins, his growing trouble with the authorities had made him a controversial and unpopular figure to many Americans. Yet it was in his own country that Ali had to win decisively and to demonstrate in the United States his domination of world boxing which he had shown abroad.

His next challenger, his fifth title defence in 1966, and his sixth within a year, was Cleveland Williams, a distinguished boxer, who, four years before this fight, was rated fifth in the world to Ali's tenth. Ali's irresistible rise — and another matter — had overtaken Williams and time was not on the challenger's side. He was thirty-three, and had passed the zenith of his prime. The other matter was that two years before Williams had been shot by a policeman in his home state of Texas. The bullet lodged in his stomach, and it was only his fine physique and condition that enabled him to pull through the operation to remove it, and to recommence his boxing career. He successfully beat three other fighters on his way to do battle with Ali, and the fight in his home state was allowed largely through civic pride as much as anything else. Those who had followed Ali's career up until the meeting with Williams possibly thought they had seen the whole gamut of the champion's weaponry, but in this fight, two new Ali characteristics

49

appeared for the first time. The first was a 'killer instinct'. All fighters must possess this if they are to succeed, and Ali undoubtedly did. But, with one or two exceptions, Ali's 'killer instinct' had been hidden beneath a mask of *laissez-faire* on the one hand and outrageous poems on the other. Against Williams, Ali gave the most impressive performance of his career, up to that time. Ali appeared not to be fighting Williams, but the whole of the United States of America. Williams was quickly reduced to a piece of flotsam caught in an astonishing whirlwind. But it was not just Ali's speed which was so impressive: it was the stunning accuracy of his ceaseless combination punches, his incessant hooks, both left and right to the head and body, his square uppercuts, the stunning jabs and the vicious, sudden, crosses. Ali took Williams apart.

In the middle of all this, Ali showed the world his second new weapon: the 'Ali Shuffle'. This boggling quickstep appeared to be fuelled by Ali's excess of adrenalin — it later became one of his most notable trademarks, but it first appeared in the fight with Williams. The second round began as the first, and it was soon obvious to all concerned — and certainly to the challenger — that nothing would stop a runaway Ali win. Williams fell to the canvas three times in the second, being saved on the last occasion from an almost certain count-out by the bell. Stretched flat on his back, Williams was dragged to his stool by his seconds, and when he came out for the third, his legs were already wobbling as he tottered towards Ali. Ali stood still, and met the challenger, and with less than half a dozen punches had floored Williams again. Williams again staggered to his feet, more from instinct than from any desire to engage Ali again, but referee Harry Kessler prevented further punishment.

And so, in his first title defence for almost a year in his own country, Ali had given the most ferocious exhibition of his tremendous ability. After the Williams fight, all America had to take Ali seriously as a boxer. Ernie Terrell, a good fighter, and a worthy challenger, had ludicrously been 'recognised' as 'champion' by the 'World' Boxing 'Association'. He visited Ali in his dressing room: "You're next!", Ali shouted. For all fight fans, the next Ali bout could not come soon enough.

(8)
February 6th 1967
v ERNIE TERRELL (USA)
venue: Astrodome, Houston, Texas
Muhammad Ali: 15st 2½lbs (212½lbs)
Ernie Terrell: 15st 2¾lbs (212¾lbs)
Referee: Harry Kessler
Attendance: 37,321

The challenge shouted out by Ali in his dressing-room to Ernie Terrell
after the win over Cleveland Williams was not just a spur-of-the-
moment gesture. Ali's troubles with the civil authorities over his draft
into the forces, had, together with his adoption of a Muslim name,
alienated a large section of the public. Among the young student
faction, however, he found some surprising support for his un-
compromising stand. Ali claimed his membership of the Nation of
Islam at a level comparable to that of a Bishop in Christian faiths
forbade him to take up arms, and therefore he would not step forward at
the induction (which would signify his acceptance of the draft). Many
famous boxers tried to get Ali to change his mind, and many more, outside of the fight game, had subjected him to continuous abuse and
criticism for his stand. Ernie Terrell had refused to acknowledge the
change in Ali's name, and pointedly always called Ali 'Cassius Clay'.
This angered Ali perhaps more than anything else, and as Terrell was at
that time preposterously put forward by the WBA as their version of the
world heavyweight champion, the fight between the two men promised
to be a real needle match.

The fight, as it transpired, was certainly that, but it was a fight to
remember in other ways. Ali's win over Cleveland Williams had been
so overwhelming in its ceaseless energy that Ali was certainly in the
finest possible physical shape for the meeting with Terrell. In addition,
the venue and referee remained the same.

Terrell came out at the start of round one with a clearly defensive line
which undoubtedly surprised Ali. Covering his face most of the time,
Terrell was able to prevent the usual jabs from Ali finding their mark,
and for the first time in Ali's career since beating Liston, Terrell proved
an opponent who more than measured up to Ali in height *and* reach.
For once, a couple of the inherent advantages which Ali almost always
seemed to possess over his opponents were absent. In these early
rounds, Terrell appeared a difficult man for Ali to beat, and, during a
particularly gritty clench in the third, Terrell later claimed that Ali
rubbed his eye on the rope while rubbing the other with his thumb.
Terrell claimed this impaired his vision for the rest of the fight. The
close in-fighting which this bout produced up to about round six again
showed a new part of Ali's multi-faceted character. Ali was perfectly

51

able to take whatever Terrell gave him (and what he allowed Terrell to land) but the close-quarter boxing, kept up round after round, made one think that the fight would go to whoever lasted longer. Almost inevitably, Ali's stamina outlasted Terrell's: but it was much more than that. After the seventh, Terrell went progressively downhill, for the vicious in-fighting and Ali's occasional dancing displays led to a tremendous left hook from Ali in that round. Terrell was visibly staggered by this punch, one of the heftiest Ali can have thrown in his career, and, after that, Terrell looked to be in trouble. The success of Ali in the seventh gave him added confidence. During the eighth round he began talking to Terrell, asking him "what's my name?", "what's my name?", repeatedly, as he gradually pulled away from his opponent on points, stamina and overall boxing craft. Ali wanted to knock Terrell out in the eighth but like Chuvalo and Mildenberger before him, he just wouldn't go. And so the familiar attrition-like battle was waged. In many ways, after the eighth, Terrell quite simply did not have a chance, and if it had not been such an important bout, it is doubtful if the referee would have allowed the slaughter to go on. For slaughter it was. Each round saw Ali scoring time and time again, a dazzling display marking the most impressive performance of his career, with Terrell being hurt painfully, obviously, pitilessly. If Ali could reduce the only challenger at the time who seemed to have any chance at all against him to this shattered creature, then he would soon be the undisputed world champion, without any boxer literally coming within striking distance.

Terrell plodded forward, flatfooted and tired, moving into the fusillade of punches from Ali. Ali was so far ahead on points at the end that the result was a mere formality: more interest was centred on Terrell's tenacity, which commanded respect, if nothing else. After the fight Ali praised Terrell's courage, but the defeated man was not there to hear the champion's acknowledgement, for he had been rushed to hospital for examination by an eye specialist. Dr Bass, Terrell's ringside doctor, said there was a blood spot on Terrell's left eyeball. The hospital, apart from examining the boxer's eyes, also had to stitch them up, for both were badly cut. The left eye had to be operated on immediately.

The referee also praised Ali's skill and prowess, claiming that the fight ended, as a contest, in the eighth. Many onlookers were shocked at Ali's taunting of the clearly outclassed Terrell by the "what's my name?" shouts, but two things must be remembered.

The first is that, with hindsight, Ali's conversion to the Islamic faith was genuine, and his change of name was a serious, fully considered, step. It was a calculated insult on Terrell's part to go out of his way to call Ali 'Cassius Clay', Ali's slave name. It was the name of the slave-owner of Ali's forefathers. To a young black, world-famous boxer or not, caught up in the burgeoning drive for civil rights and enfranchisement in the fermenting USA of the middle-sixties, the change of name was symbolic of a consciously-acquired identity. Anyone who refused to acknowledge Ali's right to assert this identity, and moreover a black who taunted him deliberately with his old slave name, was quite obviously asking for trouble. The second is that, after the Terrell slaughter, no-one called Muhammad Ali 'Cassius Clay' again.

(9)
March 22nd 1967
v ZORA FOLLEY (USA)
venue: Madison Square Garden, New York City
Muhammad Ali: 15st 1½lbs (211½lbs)
Zora Folley: 14st 6½lbs (202½lbs)
Referee: John Lobancio
Attendance: 13,708

With his wins over Cleveland Williams and Ernie Terrell, Muhammad Ali was undisputed heavyweight champion of the world. Outside events, however, were to make Ali's tenure of that office weird and brief, but for the moment he *was* the Champ, and Zora Folley his next opponent.

Folley was, in some ways, the most interesting boxer Ali had met up to that time. Folley was ageing for a boxer (he was thirty-four) and ten years before, had been regarded as a very serious contender indeed for the world heavyweight championship. For reasons which are today obscure, Folley was never allowed to try for the big prize when he was in his prime, so many felt the fight with Ali had come too late in his career. Folley, however, took his chance with a degree of preparedness which no other opponent of Ali had ever attempted.

Folley had copies of the films of all the extant Ali fights made, and studied them assiduously, noting the myriad characteristics which made up Ali's formidable ringcraft, and developing his own counter-attacks to Ali's punches. Every physical movement which the body makes is done as a result of an order being transmitted from the brain. Recent analysis has shown that the speed at which the order is transmitted (and therefore carried out) is governed by a number of factors, including habit. With a boxer (or tennis-player for that matter) the 'habit' of countering a certain type of attack can only be refined in the ring — the actuality of meeting the opponent. What was proposed was that, by sitting quietly alone, it is possible to imagine those situations (which Folley knew, for example, by studying the films) which were most likely to arise, and to imagine the response. In other words, a fight could be fought entirely in the mind, and by so doing, actually open up those lines of communication to the arms and legs with such frequency that when the time came for the fight to take place, these orders would be transmitted and received with greater speed and knowing certainty than before. It was a startling proposition, but it came to be taken up later by many distinguished athletes.

Folley himself was an extrovert character, like Ali, and amiable: when the contracts were signed, Ali expressed genuine pleasure at the thought of the coming fight — not, as so often before, in a challenging, bragging manner — happy that for the first time in his career, Folley stood to earn a lot of money from the deal. As Folley had a large family, the money was a thoroughly deserved bonus.

For all Folley's scientific approach to the contest, the fight began with Ali adopting a similar attitude to his opponent as he had with various earlier opponents: he danced around the ring, encircling Folley, with his arms hanging aimlessly by his side, defying Folley to do his worst. Although this was nothing new in Ali's career, it *was* unusual for Ali to begin a bout in this way. Folley followed Ali, lumbering along behind, and occasionally landing a punch or two on the champion's body. But this was not a fight in the class of Ali's two previous encounters: Folley had no clear answer to Ali's extraordinary attitude. Those who had paid to see a fight, along the lines of those against Cleveland Williams or Ernie Terrell, could with some justification claim they had been taken for a ride, as Ali kept up this strange exhibition of disco dancing for three rounds, pawing the air around Folley, who seemed to regard Ali's arms and legs as troublesome flies, to be brushed aside before getting on with the real business of boxing.

After this amazing opening, Ali, having so totally confused his opponent, struck a fierce right to Folley, catching him fair and square on the jaw. Ali's punch had been like a coiled spring, and Folley's reaction was as if he had been hit by a missile: he cracked to the floor, laying spread-eagled like a starfish, blood running from his nose. Amazingly, he got up, and, with powerful reserves of energy, came after Ali, with much greater determination and application than he had shown in the first eleven minutes. The respite offered between rounds revived Folley, who knew that he had it all to do with Ali. He tried to make a fight of it, and very nearly succeeded, taking the boxing to the champion, and forcing Ali to respond. The fifth and sixth rounds were much more even on points than anyone had a right to expect after the knock-down in the fourth, but in the seventh, Ali had sized Folley up in a way which needed no films. But it needed a film play-back at slow speed to confirm that Ali's right to the jaw, which hurled Folley to the floor for the second and final time, really was as fast, as accurate and as fiercely powerful as the champion claimed. Again, Folley attempted to rise, but the effort was too much, and he fell backwards, face upwards, ready to receive his seconds who rushed to drag him to the safety of his corner when the count was over. Ali had done it again.

CHAPTER SEVEN

In The Wilderness

Ali's troubles concerning his military service had now reached crisis proportions. When he registered in 1960 on reaching the age of eighteen, he had like all draftees later to take a test. The lowest mark for entry into the services was 30%. Ali had scored 16%, and was therefore ineligible for call-up. There is nothing shameful about Ali's marks: the questions required a knowledge of mathematical procedures. Here is an example:

'A shopkeeper divided a number by 3.5 when the number should have been multiplied by 4.5. His answer is 3. What should the correct number be?' (There followed four answers to choose from, three being incorrect)

Ali did not know what the correct answers were to many questions, and he did not know how to work out the problems. This is not surprising, in view of his slackness at school: when he graduated in 1960, he came 367 out of 391, and it is unlikely that anyone, on that performance, would have thought him able to pass the services' mathematical tests. Two months after taking the test, he was retested, with the same result: 16%. He was classified 1—Y, unsuitable for service.

Two events conspired to change all that: the first was Ali's membership of the Black Muslims, coupled with holding the world heavyweight championship. The second was that many clever young men, knowing the pass mark was 30%, deliberately did badly in the examinations to avoid military service. As the United States involvement in the Vietnam war was escalating greatly, and more soldiers were needed the ludicrous situation arose whereby an estimated 20,000 university graduates had been exempted from service for failing the tests.

The government acted: the pass mark was halved and reduced from 30% to 15%. This automatically made Ali's previous 16% failure a pass mark — by one per cent. He was reclassified 1-A (suitable for service) without further examination. Ali appealed against the re-classification on three points: he was a conscientious objector, a minister of a religion (the Black Muslim leader Elijah Muhammad declared him to be the equivalent of a Bishop), and as a man with a family he would suffer financial hardship if forced to join the armed forces. His stand, coupled with the escalation of the Vietnam war, led to a fierce reaction against him. His boasting had been bad enough, but now he was regarded by many people as a traitor. Cities refused to grant licenses for Ali fights, which explains the number of fights in Europe and Canada during 1966.

On April 26th 1967, a little over a month after his fight with Zora

Folley, Ali reported for induction at the Armed Forces Induction Center, in Houston, Texas. He refused to step forward (which would have signified his acceptance) when his name was called: the day before his lawyers had filed a lengthy petition to the Federal Court.

That day, within hours of Ali leaving the Center, the New York Boxing Commission withdrew recognition of Ali's world championship title. The same day the World Boxing Association did likewise, and on June 26th Ali was found guilty of unlawfully refusing induction. He was fined $10,000 and sentenced to five years imprisonment.

With an arrogance which took the breath away, two United States boxing organisations, without waiting for the courts to decide the legality of Ali's refusal to be drafted, stripped this clear world champion of his title. Ali's refusal to fight for his country was taken as a public insult: it was not. Few could appreciate that being heavyweight champion of the world did not mean Ali possessed a commensurate willingness to kill people. Perhaps if Ali had been world chess champion, or a world-class violinist, the extraordinary animosity would not have been aroused. Playing chess or the violin are not physically dangerous: one cannot get killed following either pursuit, although some chess enthusiasts and music-lovers might wish otherwise. Boxing stood for aggression, physical domination — what right had the champion to declare himself a pacifist? In fact, as the Supreme Court finally ruled, Ali had every right.

Two questions remain unanswered: the first is that Ali was by no means the only prominent young American not to become enlisted in the armed forces of the United States at that time. Film actors and pop stars somehow eluded the draft. Many of the most forceful young protestors in song were themselves without the experience of that which they so vehemently protested against. Few rock stars, sportsmen or film actors went to jail for not being drafted. Ali however, did not evade the issue: he refused to be inducted and refused the many easy options which were offered to him. Many highly tempting deals were proposed: among them, he could have joined the army, remained in the USA, been allowed full training facilities, and kept his title. But he turned them down flat. His religious beliefs, however offensive or unacceptable they were to some people, were the overriding consideration for him. His intransigence had already led to the break-up of his marriage: it also led to the withdrawal of the thing he wanted most of all.

The other question is by what right do American organisations strip an athlete of a world title? Ali was *world* champion — he had beaten the champions of Canada, Britain, Germany, the United States and other territories. He was champion of champions, and his contenders were drawn from countries far removed from the United States. Whatever internal problems were encountered in the USA, these had nothing whatsoever to do with world boxing. The actions of the American boxing authorities were arrogant, selfish, immoral, illegal, and ultimately pathetic. Could Hitler have stripped Max Schmelling of his title if he had criticised the Third Reich? Could Mussolini have removed Primo Carnera's title if he had fallen foul of the *fascisti*? Imagine the outcry in the 'Land of the Free' if one or both of these things had happened! Furthermore, it was hypocrisy of the most hideous kind for those who claimed Ali's action subverted the youth of America, when earlier title-holders (and current contenders) had openly associated with mobsters, known killers and organised crime.

The late 1960s marked a watershed in the history of the United States, and the Muhammad Ali story was a small part of the incredible state of flux in which the country found itself. The Vietnam war was a turning-point in world events: the USA suffered the first defeat in its history, and after Vietnam the country could never be the same again. For the USA does not have a 'United States' to fall back on. For better or worse, the countries of the western world rely, either militarily or economically, on the umbrella-like protection of the USA. If the USA crumbles, then western democracy is finished. The Vietnam war raises the question whether the youth of America would flock to the flag with the same degree of enthusiasm which their forefathers had shown, should the country consider the principles for which it stands to be under attack in the future.

Ali appealed against his conviction, and while this dragged on through the courts he was effectively barred from boxing. The circumstances of the withdrawal of his title recognition meant that no city was willing to allow him to fight by granting him a licence. The reasons given for not granting him a licence were, in retrospect, absurd: the New York Athletic Commission refused because of their policy of refusing to grant a licence to anyone convicted of a felony who had not served his sentence. A lawyer employed by the National Association for the Advancement of Coloured People pointed out that the New York Commission had granted boxing licences to 90 fighters convicted of embezzlement, rape and murder. The more telling observation was made in Ali's defence, on a point of law which all democratic countries can understand:

'Freedom on bail implies the right of a defendent to pursue his normal occupation while awaiting court settlement over the case.'

But it was all to no avail: no mayor, no governor, was willing to risk the political hot potato of granting Ali a licence. Unable to work, Ali's time was spent at home with his second wife, whom he married on August 19th 1967, and he embarked on a new career as lecturer to university campuses, student gatherings and other organisations. Within a short time he had become one of the most sought-after speakers in the country. His financial situation had deteriorated, naturally, but although his circumstances were reduced, his previous earnings enabled him to enjoy a reasonable standard of living. With his passport withdrawn, a normal procedure for those on bail, he could not leave the country to fight abroad.

Just before Christmas 1968, Ali was jailed for ten days for nonpayment of a fine for a traffic offence the previous year. The experience in jail was vivid and degrading, but in the event he only served eight days, being released for a Christmas amnesty. As far as most of the public were concerned, however, Ali was still champion. When, three months after stripping Ali of his title, the WBA commenced a series of fights to find the new champion, public demonstrations and picketing of offices and venues showed what the public thought of the charade.

Ali's career as champion naturally led to speculation as to how good he really was, in comparison with the giants of the past. Technology could provide some kind of answer, and a few businessmen persuaded Ali and other fighters to agree to participate in 'computer'-fights, whereby known data on each boxer was fed into the computers, which then predicted the outcome of a likely fight between two chosen fighters. It was a novel and tempting idea, and in one Ali was 'defeated' by James J. Jeffries (a decision which upset him greatly — he filed a $500,000 suit for damages), and a filmed fight against Rocky Marciano. Several possible endings were filmed, with neither fighter knowing which one was chosen by the computer. Marciano never discovered, for he was killed in a plane crash a few weeks later. The computer 'chose' Marciano as the victor, knocking Ali out in round thirteen. Ali was unhappy at the film — not so much by the decision which was highly probable as a prediction — as by the promoters: he felt both he and Marciano had been misled. He denounced the film in public, and by so doing led Sugar Ray Robinson to withdraw from another film planned in the series. The promoters sued Ali. He also appeared on Broadway, in a black musical called *Big Time Buck White*. Ali admitted the show was bad, for it folded after a couple of weeks, but he added, "I was great".

Gradually, however, the pressure on the authorities, and the growing awareness of the basically unconstitutional treatment suffered by Ali, together with the rise of the anti-Vietnam war movement, led to a shift of opinion in his favour. The Supreme Court ruled that a man's religious beliefs entitled him to be a conscientious objector.

Finally, after a great deal of string-pulling, heartaches, broken promises, despair, false hopes and hopelessness, the city of Atlanta, Georgia, granted Ali a licence to fight. The opponent was naturally to be Joe Frazier, who had emerged as world champion following the internal wrangling of the various boxing factions in the USA, but, in the heat of the action, no-one had actually bothered to ask Frazier if he was free to fight on the date set aside for the fight. He was not, having a contract to fight another boxer only a week or so after the Ali date. Without wishing to lose this priceless opportunity, Ali's helpers quickly found another fighter — Jerry Quarry. While Ali was training for this fight, the New York Supreme Court ruled that Ali must be given a licence to fight in that city. Ali was on the way back, but he had only six weeks in which to get ready.

CHAPTER EIGHT

The Way Back

(1)
October 27th 1970
v JERRY QUARRY (USA)
venue: Municipal Auditorium, Atlanta, Georgia
Muhammad Ali: 15st 3lbs (213lbs)
Jerry Quarry: 14st 1½lbs (197½lbs)
Referee: Tony Perez
Attendance: 5,000

Few post-war fights have ever been as eagerly awaited as this, the return to the professional ring after more than three-and-a-half years by Muhammad Ali. Although, as we have seen, he had been stripped of his title, he had not lost it in the ring, and for many people, Ali was still the 'real' champion. However, he had to go through a number of preliminary bouts before he could meet Joe Frazier for a fight which would determine the undisputed heavyweight champion of the world. In the event, Ali's return to the professional boxing ring was as complete a triumph as anyone could have wished: it seemed as though, amazingly, he had picked up the threads of his career where he was obliged to leave it all that time before. There are those who believe that Quarry was not entirely up to the task, but they are surely mistaken: Quarry was indeed a worthy opponent, with a distinguished record, powerful determination and skill. For Quarry, it was a golden opportunity, not just to fight the legendary Muhammad Ali, but to have the chance to beat him. Many also felt that Ali's years away from the ring would have proved his downfall — that he had paid the price for his insistence on his religious principles by being so out of condition and rusty in experience as to make his return a farce.

Ali again dumbfounded his critics, and the first round of this contest must, surely, be among the most outstanding demonstrations by Ali in the whole of his career. From the start, Ali appeared to have lost none of his old speed and manner, but this was allied to a fierce killer-instinct, which had only been seen before to this degree in the fight against Cleveland Williams. Ali's speed was dazzling, and his jabs were as accurate and as proliferating as ever. He blocked and countered Quarry's far from negligible bombs, in one move so outwitting his opponent that Ali's left glove seemed to become swallowed up in the splodgy skin of Quarry's face. Quarry was shaken by this — as well he might have been — but his speed was lethargic in the extreme by comparison with the charismatic Ali. In the second minute it appeared as though the fight would soon be over when Ali caught him with four successive lefts to the head, which rocked Quarry, who stood transfixed, unable to move, totally caught flatfooted by the barrage.

In the opening round Quarry's left eyebrow had been cut: according to Quarry, this came about through a clash of heads, but the film of the fight disproves this. Quarry had managed to force Ali on to the ropes during the round, and the cut arose from a retaliatory right cross from Ali. After the tremendous energy of the first round, the second began on the same high level. Soon after it began, Ali landed three left jabs and a half right which connected with Quarry's chin. Quarry, in reply, attacked as best he could, but almost always his blows were fended off by Ali's powerful forearms. In short, Ali totally prevented Quarry from getting near him, so his opponent was virtually unable to hurt or mark Ali. As the third round began, Ali danced again around Quarry, but not quite as quickly as he had been able to at the outset of his championship career. The opening thirty seconds of this round was the only time when Ali's absence from the ring and his advancing years appeared to be catching up with him, but this was just a momentary thought as Ali reduced the fight to a farce. During Ali's prancing around he proferred no punches or attack at all to Quarry, who was able to seize the moment with a left to Ali's body of considerable force. Ali backed on to the ropes, away from trouble, to catch his breath, and then, demonstrating his big reach advantage, put his hand on Quarry's head, keeping his opponent at bay with the simplest of tactics. Ali knew he had his man, and caught Quarry's head with a jarring right which recalled the onslaught of the opening round. Quarry was clearly shaken but in retaliation forced Ali back on the ropes again by sheer strength. Ali, however, knowing his opponent had been roused by his action, landed a winding, fierce left to the stomach, followed by another searing right to Quarry's head: they fell into a clinch and when Tony Perez separated the men it was clear that Quarry's head was badly cut. The bell ended further damage, but during the interval Quarry's trainer knew his man could take no more of this: the referee, called to Quarry's corner, ended the fight.

It was a tremendous performance by Ali, the most superb come-back he could possibly have wished for. It seemed that his great qualities had not been impaired by his absence from the ring, and it also seemed a cast-iron certainty that, given the chance, Muhammad Ali would be the undisputed and still undefeated heavyweight champion of the world. After the fight, some revealing comments from Angelo Dundee showed just how much was at stake. He said, admitting that he was worried as to the effects of Ali's long lay-off: "when the first jab went in solidly I knew it was all right." In view of Ali's unstoppable, overwhelming performance in the first round, Dundee's comment would seem a little understated, but Ali himself admitted that he found Quarry a difficult man to catch with his bobbing and weaving. He frankly owned up that he missed Quarry with some punches because he was so elusive. It seemed, however momentary, that Ali's revolutionary approach to heavyweight boxing was being taken up by his contemporaries and that, as time went on, Ali might just come up against a younger, faster man. That would indeed be a fight, but for Quarry, then and there, his facial damage was serious enough to have eleven stitches in the wound.

(2)
December 7th 1970
v OSCAR BONAVENA (ARGENTINA)
venue: Madison Square Garden, New York City
Muhammad Ali: 15st 2lbs (212lbs)
Oscar Bonavena: 14st 8lbs (204 lbs)
Referee: Mark Conn
Attendance: 19,417

There was little doubt, after Ali's tremendous win over Jerry Quarry, that he would have to have a couple more fights before meeting Joe Frazier, but some of Ali's staunchest supporters were a little taken aback at the choice of Oscar Bonavena for only his second fight after such a long lay-off.

Bonavena was an immensely strong and powerful boxer, who had never been stopped in his 53 professional fights. He had, moreover, the distinction of having gone the distance twice with Joe Frazier, and in turn had knocked Frazier down on two occasions. Bonavena was a formidable opponent, indeed, but, amazingly, he was the one who started the pre-match verbal slanging. Bonavena called Ali a coward, a chicken and much else besides, and it was Ali who was forced to adopt the air of nonchalance when confronted by Bonavena's outbursts. Curiously enough, Bonavena's tantrums had the effect on Ali of winding him up to a pitch of revenge. Before the fight Ali proclaimed with deadly seriousness that he never wanted to beat a man so badly. "The Beast is mine. Tonight he falls in nine."

The fight began: Ali was invincible in the opening rounds, his speed and persistent left jabs made it appear as though this was to be yet another victory along the lines of those familiar successes in the past. But Bonavena was not quite the same kind of opponent as Ali's earlier adversaries. He was unorthodox, being able to duck quickly, and at times he matched Ali's legendary speed of reflex. Consequently, although Ali dominated the first three rounds, Bonavena was quite able to take the fight to Ali at close quarters on more than one occasion, a tactic which was certainly not attempted by Jerry Quarry. It may be that this surprising counter-attack by Bonavena, which enabled him to land several stinging blows to Ali's body, made Ali realise that he had more of a fight on his hands than he possibly had bargained for. In the fourth, Bonavena came back at Ali, and for the first time the American looked surprisingly flat-footed as he retreated to the ropes, unable to dance away as in days gone by. Bonavena followed him, and began piling blows into Ali's body and around his head. Ali could do little, it appeared, to counter this barrage, and he stood and took a great deal of punishment. For the first time in his career, Ali began to look rusty and old: but was this true, or was it some fiendish ploy on his part to lull Bonavena into a false sense of security? If the latter was indeed his method, then it was a painful and dangerous game to play, but it seemed inconceivable that Ali could be in danger. His speed had not entirely left him, but Bonavena kept hitting, jabbing and pushing Ali with more frequency, and Ali swapped punches with him in a brawling, battling style that disconcerted his more transient admirers.

This was a side of Ali's personality which had not been seen before in the ring: he was, in many rounds of this fight, a slugger, a prizefighter of the old heavyweight school, unwilling or unable — but more than likely unprepared — to move away from the solid Argentinian as of old. The crowd could not believe it: there was little ringcraft, little skill, no finesse, no sudden changes of pace and variety of attack by either boxer. Surely this could not be Muhammad Ali? Yes, it was, but it was also Oscar Bonavena. The Argentinian's iron determination, his relentless drive, his astonishing capacity to take punishment and still come after more showed quite clearly that Ali, in his preparations for this fight, had seriously underestimated his opponent and had possibly not trained as well as he should have. Ali, his energy depleted by his lack of application, found himself forced back on his natural inner strength as he was made to slug it out, punch for punch, round after round, against the seemingly indomitable Bonavena. This was hardly what the crowd wanted, but it was what they got: a fight in the old manner. In round nine, the one in which Ali had rashly predicted Bonavena would be knocked out, Ali exerted a tremendous amount of energy and might in an attempt to make his prediction come true. He threw a massive left hook at Bonavena which just missed the Argentinian, but the force and velocity of Ali's punch toppled him to his knee, as Ali slipped and fell momentarily. The crowd was in uproar, as Bonavena caught Ali with a terrifying hook which numbed and jarred Ali. The brute force and trenchant punching of both men continued with unremitting fury until the bell — and after it, for both men were so intent on their task they never heard it ring. If the crowd thought the fight had gone downhill after the fourth, then round nine surely was the logical conclusion to this style of fighting. Strength and stamina were the two ingredients on the physical side, but mentally, determination was the only factor. Both men had obviously exerted themselves immensely in the ninth, and the following five rounds never rose to the heights again. Ali had failed in his prediction (not for the first time) and the fight continued on its tough, abrupt and massive way.

However spirited Bonavena's opposition had been to Ali, it was clear that the American was leading on points, so only a late knockout could turn the fight Bonavena's way. The final round began, therefore, with all to play for, but it was Ali who provided the finishing touch of ferocity. Towards the end of the first minute, Ali caught Bonavena with a disploding left hook which connected with Bonavena's chin. He went down, but almost immediately got up again, and rushed furiously at Ali, for all the world as if to punish him for this humiliating upset. But Bonavena's legs could no longer do what his rational mind wanted, and Ali caught him on the run with another left hook which felled him like a wounded polar bear. At the count of eight, Bonavena struggled gamely to his feet, and Ali, his adrenalin flowing at high speed, furiously pounded Bonavena's head and body with a combination of left and right hooks — only a few were needed to put him down for a third time. Under New York Boxing Commission rules, three knock-downs in one round constitute a technical knockout and Ali had won. No matter where the fight had been staged, he would have finally overcome the tremendously strong and savagely perpetual Bonavena.

It was the first time Bonavena had ever been knocked out: after the fight, in his broken English, the Argentinian recanted: speaking of Ali, he said "This the champion. Frazier never win him. I never go down before, never."

In spite of the ringside reports of a comparatively lack-lustre Ali who was possibly under-prepared, this was, in its own way, a great fight. There is no doubt, as Ali later admitted with disarming frankness, that he had gravely underestimated his opponent. In the ring, confronted with something much bigger and more difficult than he ever imagined, Ali forced himself to beat the man on sheer strength alone. It speaks volumes for his capacity that he was, with only one previous fight after over three-and-a-half years away from professional fighting, able to defeat this truly formidable boxer. There was no time for horseplay in this, the most tremendous and physical of all Ali's fights up to then. Ali showed he could take it, and he could also dish it out, and Bonavena was forced to admit the Kentuckian's superiority.

The lessons from this fight for Ali were obvious: he had to train as never before to recover his strength and reflexes (in so far as reflexes can ever be recovered), if he was to overwhelm Joe Frazier. He could no longer take so many things for granted. Few doubted that he would soon regain that which was taken from him by the Lilliputians, but he would need to look to his training rather more than he appeared to have done against Bonavena.

(3)
March 8th 1971
v JOE FRAZIER (USA) HEAVYWEIGHT
CHAMPION OF THE WORLD
venue: Madison Square Garden, New York City
Muhammad Ali: 15st 5lbs (215lbs)
Joe Frazier: 14st 9½lbs (205½lbs)
Referee: Arthur Mercante
Attendance: 20,455

The fights between Muhammad Ali and Joe Frazier will cause boxing enthusiasts to haggle forever. All three meetings are preserved on film and remain as remarkable documents of the boxing skills of both men. In retrospect it is clear that Ali's preparations for their first meeting were insufficient. The reasons for this are manifold and interacting. The first is Ali's state of mind after his second successive win following his return. As we have seen, his first win, over Jerry Quarry, was complete and utterly convincing, clearly the result of thorough preparation (in the time available) and a determined effort to win well. It could well have been that this defeat of Quarry caused him to think that things had not changed much since he was barred from boxing. If he thought that way, he was largely right, but the win itself, and his underestimation of Bonavena, caused him immense problems in his fight with the Argentinian. Ali overcame these problems, as we have seen, but at great personal cost and effort. The important thing to remember as the first Frazier fight approached, was that Ali, in knocking out Bonavena, had done the very thing which Frazier had manifestly failed to do on two occasions. Furthermore, Bonavena had taken Frazier to within a whisker of defeat. Surely Ali must have thought that if he could have beaten Bonavena in such circumstances, then Frazier would be a somewhat easier opponent.

It is highly significant that the 'old-time' school of fighter, epitomised by Sonny Liston, was as dead and buried as if from a previous century. By 1971 the civil rights movement had won most of its major battles, the Vietnam war was coming to an end, and the national identity of the blacks in America had assumed a far greater sense of pride and nobility since the upheavals of the previous decade. Sonny Liston himself had dropped from sight after the two fights with Ali: he found himself banned from boxing for a time, reduced to deplorable circumstances, and was found dead in his bed on December 30th 1970. The autopsy revealed he had taken an overdose of drugs and he had been dead for ten or eleven days before his corpse was discovered.

Frazier had several of the old 'Cassius Clay' characteristics. Like Ali, Frazier was intelligent, and had earned a lot of money from his fighting and other activities. He even pursued a career as a rock singer, with a group called the Knockouts, although his singing was little better than

Ali's. In addition, Frazier had beaten every fighter set before him as champion, and his skull was famed for its apparent insensitivity. Fighters would break their fists on Frazier's cranium: the blows meant nothing to him. He is reputed to have bathed his head in cold salt water every day to harden the skin, but whatever the reason, he was an incredibly tough character.

Frazier and Ali enjoyed a good personal rapport: they were friends, each respecting the other. Frazier had named his son after Ali — a great compliment. Even though Frazier was the official world champion, and had defended his crown with conspicuous success, there was one man forever at his shoulder. Frazier, for all his wins, was still an unknown figure, whereas Ali, not at that time holding any title, was an international figure whose charismatic drawing-power was superior to that of any other boxer. There was no way that Frazier could sleep soundly in his bed at nights until he had licked Ali.

And so the protagonists squared-off against each other. On the one hand, Ali, desperate to regain the title, his spirits high after his wins over Quarry and Bonavena. He had done to Bonavena what Frazier had failed to do. Surely he must prevail over Frazier? Frazier stood on the other hand: an honourable man, a thinking fighter, very tough indeed, already world champion. He had a lot to lose. In fact, neither fighter could afford to lose this one, billed as 'The Fight of the Century'. The prospect became the highest-paid boxing match ever. Both men received two and a half million dollars purse money.

The fight began with tremendous drama. Frazier had obviously learned from Bonvena's unconventional approach to Ali's speed and jabs, for, like the Argentinian, Frazier was able to take the fight to Ali in the opening rounds, in spite of Ali's dancing and light footwork, by slipping round and under Ali's incessant jabs. In the opening round Frazier caught Ali with a sickening left hook to the head which clearly staggered Ali, and slowed him a lot sooner than he was expecting. Ali, in turn, was able to sway away from most of Frazier's many shots to the head. The first round was undoubtedly Frazier's and the powerful drama continued into the second, with Frazier still out-manoeuvering — rather too many times for Ali's comfort — the challenger's jabs and hooks. On balance, this was also Frazier's round, and in the third Ali surprised the distinguished onlookers by going straight on to the ropes, even before Frazier had come after him, adopting a defensive position. For whatever reason, this was not the most sensible of tactics: Frazier could get close to Ali, in spite of Ali's eight inches superiority in reach, and the champion landed a whole succession of blows to Ali's body which must have hurt. In short, in these opening rounds, Frazier was fighting a tremendous match, out-flanking Ali, whose lack of sustained application in training was now becoming apparent to all. In the third, as if to play down any danger the crowd might imagine him to be in, Ali shook his head at the onlookers, as if to reassure them that Frazier's attacks meant nothing. It was an extraordinary spectacle, but those who had seen Frazier fight before knew that he had no reason to throw anything less than his heaviest punches at Ali. The fourth round was also Frazier's: he kept up an incessant attack at Ali, who, for whatever reason, still refused to keep out of harm's way. It seemed, almost with disbelief in the eyes of those watching the fight, as though Ali really had lost his youthful spring and pep, and, unbelievably, was only able to stand there and soak up Frazier's far from negligible punishment. After the fight, Frazier paid Ali some great compliments, especially recalling his refusal to be swayed by the barrage, and this continued into round five. By this time, it was clear that Frazier had built up a good lead, one which Ali would have the greatest difficulty in overcoming, but only those Ali supporters — and there were many — who were willing to put up with anything from their hero, were able to keep faith with Ali by assuming that this was all part of some careful ploy. If so, it was a dangerous game to play, and the stakes were too high to permit any mistake. Few could really believe the disdain with which Ali appeared to be treating the punishment which, for most other fighters, would have been almost too much to take. In the sixth, Ali suddenly took the offensive from Frazier, and attacked the legendary skull of leather and steel, actually drawing blood from the champion's eyes and mouth. This was what the Ali fans wanted: surely this would mark the turn of the tide? In a sense it did, for Ali was able to score effectively with his jabs, as Frazier appeared momentarily disconcerted by Ali's sudden change of pace. But Frazier in round eight soon brushed aside Ali's temporary advantage by a fierce attack. Ali instinctively kept away from Frazier, but those who had followed the pre-match stories of Ali's laziness in training were now hoping against hope that their man could pull it out of the hat. Ali had predicted that Frazier would go in round six, but that was long past, and seemed in retrospect to be one rash guess too often for the Louisville Lip, who, incredibly, in the eighth, offered no attack whatsoever (worth mentioning) to Frazier. Ali just stood there, dancing around occasionally, his hands at his sides like a jerky puppet, unconcerned at the deadly danger from the Blackamoor facing Ali's Petrushka. In the ninth, Ali jabbed and jabbed again at Frazier, another startling change of tactics, but the big man was not to be deflected from his course by Ali's chameleon-like display of how to box, and how not to box. Then, suddenly, like a brilliant sun blazing across a black void, Ali caught Frazier with three successive left and right combinations to the head, but the sun had blazed too late in the round. Frazier was visibly shaken by this, his legs uncertain in their gait, and his eyes glazed as much in anger and disbelief as from the shock to his nervous system. The bell intervened, and Frazier was able to recover in the interval, for at the start of the tenth, he erupted from his corner as if propelled: Ali caught him with a tremendous punch, and then himself swayed back on the ropes. The crowd caught the tension of this electrifying moment and Frazier appeared to be near the end of the fight. Several times, Ali caught Frazier again and again in the round, but Frazier, for all the punishment he was obliged to take, did not go down. The round was definitely Ali's: a tremendous round, but a mere prelude to that which followed. The eleventh round was unforgettable. As if reaching into the very depths of his being, Frazier attacked Ali with a ferocity and dedication that were awe-inspiring to behold: a massive left to the body of Ali caught him and sent him quickly floorwards — it was so sudden that at first it was thought to be a slip on Ali's part, but the film disproves that. Ali was bent double with the force of Frazier's punches and was sent staggering backwards to the ropes. Ali, roused by this slugging attack, countered with a powerful right to Frazier, and, to the crowd's utter disbelief, actually waved Frazier back, as though to motion him away: not out of fear or cowardice, but to show him that the attack meant nothing to him. Ali's sheer courage commanded respect, but Frazier was not to be denied by this effrontery: he came forward, remorselessly, and caught a thunderous blow to Ali's jaw. Ali reeled, but refused to go down, much to his corner's surprise, for a bucket of water was thrown in an attempt to catch Ali and to revive him. Completely against the rules, this instinctive reaction by Ali's corner later earned a severe reprimand. In such colossal tension did this remarkable round end.

In the nature of things, the succeeding rounds could only be regarded as an anticlimax after the titanic struggle of the eleventh. For Ali, shaken and as close to exhaustion as at any time in his career, moved into Frazier at every opportunity, clinching and holding as much as possible, resisting attempts to separate them: but Frazier, too, was far from fresh. He had used almost all his energy in the eleventh round, but he still tried with what reserves remained to carry what was left of the fight to Ali. Ali, during the twelfth, thirteenth and fourteenth rounds, had begun to realise the herculean task which confronted him, but it was seemingly not within his power to undertake it, at such a late stage, and with his energy depleted. The Final Round: the men came out, touched gloves, and the last three minutes of this struggle were under way. Both, from wherever such reserves are buried, drew on fresh energy for the final summit. Frazier, still, amazingly, kept up his constant harassment of Ali, who, also amazingly, found energy to move and to occasionally bob and weave away from Frazier's blows. Ali was not finished yet: knowing he had to knock Frazier out in the final round, as he had achieved against Bonavena, Ali drew his right arm back, almost as far as it would go, to obtain the maximum force and velocity. Frazier saw the danger and stepped in, across the trajectory of Ali's intended punch, to land a cracking left hook which caught Ali at his most exposed and vulnerable. His right leg folded, and his straight left leg did nothing to ease his fall to the floor. By no mistake was this a slip: Ali had been felled by a crossing left, just as Henry Cooper had caught him almost eight years before. Ali's shoulders hit the canvas, his feet in the air, but such was the unusual nature of the experience that instead of remaining down for a count of eight to recover his bearings, he almost instinctively jumped up again at two. Frazier himself was dog-tired, and even though both men, their forces spent, still managed to aim, and occasionally land, blows to each other's heads in the closing minutes of the round, Ali — not without a certain understandable connivance from Frazier — managed to hold his opponent rather more than referee Mercante could have allowed in earlier rounds. At the final bell, almost inaudible beneath the welter of sound from the audience, both men fell into each other's arms, utterly exhausted, worn out, but secure in the knowledge that, on the night, they had both given all they had.

It was clear, if such things are clear at all, that the fight was Frazier's: he had won a tremendous victory, and had fought a superb battle, exploiting those chinks in Ali's armour which had been evident for many years, but which were compounded by his protracted absence from the ring, his greater age, his loss of speed, but most of all by his own imagined invincibility. If Muhammad Ali had trained and prepared himself as thoroughly for this fight as he should have done, and indeed as Frazier so clearly had, then the result might well have been different.

And so Ali's unprecedented unbeaten career came to an end that night. He had failed to regain the heavyweight championship of the world, and for once the Mouth had been silenced. But Frazier's win, of course, was infinitely more than that. Frazier had been damaged by Ali in the fight: his indomitable style had caused him to take many straight punches on the face and body, and his face was very badly swollen, especially around both eyes. There were no hard feelings on either side after the match. Frazier said of Ali: "He's a good man. He's hard to beat. I was amazed at what he took. I tell you, I went right back home to get those shots that I finally got him with." The demeanour of both men — both Olympic medal-winners in their time — after the fight was exemplary.

In a curious way, the defeat did Ali a great deal of good, for most importantly, in the eyes of the vast majority of the public who knew little of boxing but certainly knew of Muhammad Ali, his defeat showed he was human, after all.

A few weeks later, Joe Frazier was admitted to hospital in Philadelphia. He was suffering from emotional and physical exhaustion, and needed complete convalescence. At the same time, Ali was beginning preparations for his next fight, which was scheduled for four months' time. There were those who still felt that, although he may have lost to Frazier in the ring on the night, Ali was the ultimate victor, who still stalked Frazier outside the ring. The matter was still undecided, and only a second meeting would begin to answer the unanswered questions.

CHAPTER NINE

Detour

(1)
July 26th 1971
v JIMMY ELLIS (USA)
venue: Astrodome, Houston, Texas
Muhammad Ali: 15st 10½lbs (220½lbs)
Jimmy Ellis: 13st 7 lbs (189lbs)
Referee: Jay Edson
Attendance: 32,000

The nature of the defeat of Muhammad Ali by Joe Frazier meant that Ali's plans to stride back into the heavyweight chair which he had been forced to vacate out of the ring had taken a sharp about-turn. While a rematch with Frazier was almost certain, Ali would naturally have to maintain his momentum and keep up his ring experience with a number of other fights, which, almost incidentally, would help remove a few rival contenders *en route*.

In the internal fiasco which raged after the various boxing authorities had stripped Muhammad Ali of his world title in 1967, Jimmy Ellis, Ali's one-time sparring partner, had emerged as the official heavyweight champion. He lost the title to Frazier, but Ellis was naturally anxious to regain it. He was a highly intelligent boxer, with many superb skills, quiet, 'together' in the best sense, and keen, now that Frazier had beaten Ali, to show that the 1,000-odd sparring rounds he had gone with Ali in training meant he knew more about his opponent than any other boxer. Ellis was in the front rank of contenders to fight Frazier, so a match with Ali was a good draw. As he also came from the Angelo Dundee school, the fight would be fascinating, a glimpse of opposing skills, and, interestingly enough, Dundee agreed to train Ellis for the fight against Ali. Harry Wiley, who had trained Sugar Ray Robinson, among others, stood in for Dundee.

Ellis's background in the fight game had been very similar to Ali's and there was a great connexion between the two men. They had grown up in Louisville together and Ellis maintained he had defeated Cassius Clay as an amateur. But that had been a very long time ago, and if Ellis claimed the 1,000 rounds with Ali gave him an advantage over other opponents, the reverse was also true: Ali had fought 1,000 rounds with *him*, and knew *his* style as no other boxer. Whatever was to happen, the fight could hold few surprises for either man.

Ellis had clearly studied the nature of Frazier's win, and the approach of Bonavena, for he came into the fight with a tremendous discharge of energy in the opening round, matching Ali's famous speed of old, and landing several telling punches on Ali's head and body. Ali, however, had literally seen all this before, and appeared unconcerned at Ellis's attack. It soon appeared that Ali had trained with greater application for this fight than he had shown in the Frazier preparations, as his movements had a sprightlier step to them, a greater accuracy of kelk. The second and third rounds were more even, with Ellis a little slower, choosing his moments with greater appreciation for their likely effectiveness, and Ali, too, appearing more relaxed and powerful, bobbing and dancing, seeking a momentary lapse of concentration to exploit.

The fourth round was decisive: a massive right from Ali caught Ellis by surprise (in Ellis's own words "it sneaked up on me") and severely hurt him. Ali did not press home this chance as he might have done, and as he certainly would have done had the opponent been anyone other than Ellis. But Ellis was clearly shaken by this blow, and only just managed to finish the round on his feet. During the interval Dundee had worked well to revive the boxer, and it does seem that the 'family' style of the bout affected the manner in which it was fought. With Ali and Ellis, old sparring partners and buddies, with Dundee himself in Ellis's corner, and with Ali knowing full well that the fourth round left hook had seriously weakened his opponent, it would have been rather less than honourable if Ali had then set about destroying Ellis's career — as he very likely could have done. This is not to underestimate Ellis, but to see things in their correct perspective. After all, Ellis held no title for Ali to win: there was no need to demonstrate any physical superiority over Ellis, and the one thing that *was* required — a public demonstration of Ali's ability to go twelve rounds — could be accomplished without inflicting undue damage to Ellis. This, at least, is how Dundee saw Ali's handling of the fight afterwards, and the fight became, after round four, a rather superb exhibition match, with delightful changes of pace and rhythm, methods of attack, pushing forward, probing, pulling back, use of the ropes, spacing, distance, timing — all these things made Ali appear a pluperfect boxer in the fight, a superb craftsman, totally in command of himself — and his opponent. Finally, in the last round, the twelfth, Ali again connected an eruptive left bolo to Ellis's jaw, continuing with several right-left-right combinations. Ellis was beaten, lolling against the ropes, but Ali (almost mercifully) did not seek to knock him out. The referee stepped between them, and signalled Ellis to his corner, raising Ali's left arm in victory.

It was an unusual win for Ali: not as insignificant as some felt, for Ali obviously sought a good win after his defeat by Frazier, and Ellis, after all, had been world champion at one time. But Ali's killer instinct, a part of his make-up as any other, and one which had on occasion been fearsomely exhibited in the ring, was here absent, until, in the last round, Ali dispatched his man with clinical ease, and, almost, humanity.

(2)
November 17th 1971
v BUSTER MATHIS (USA)
venue: Astrodome, Houston, Texas
Muhammad Ali: 16st 3 lbs (227lbs)
Buster Mathis: 18st 4lbs (256lbs)
Referee: Earl Keel
Attendance: 15,000

If Ali's fight with Jimmy Ellis had shown some faintly disappointing features, this fight with Buster Mathis carried the somewhat negative side of Ali's nature a stage further.

A glance at the statistics above tells most of the story: at 227lbs Ali weighed in at the heaviest he had ever been, but even so, he was giving 29lbs to his opponent. Mathis's weight was enormous, but rather too much of it was constituted of flab for comfort, and, like Ali, he himself was returning to the ring after a 30-month lay-off, following an over-whelming defeat by Jerry Quarry. Mathis was clearly out of condition and lacked sharpness and energy. The fight has been called a farce (although parts of the Frazier fight could be tagged with that noun) but it was not entirely without merit.

The fight meant something to Mathis, who tried, sometimes des-perately, to show that he could make a respectable showing in the ring against Ali, still one of the most formidable fighters around. Ali, however, began the fight as he used to of old: he circled his man, sizing him up, jabbing (not as speedily as in the sixties) and moving out of danger just when his opponent seemed poised for something or other. Over the first four rounds, Ali gradually built up a points lead, but, whereas in the old days he would have suddenly erupted and clinched the fight, in this one (as before with Ellis) he seemed bereft of the killer instinct. He was content to coast along at times, completely in control of the fight, not to test the temperature, more to take it easy, relax, calm down any dramatic moment which might arise. Ali seemed concerned to remove tension, layer by layer, from the bout: a totally new type of boxing match. Ali was in no danger of losing, and appeared intent to use the fight, as with Ellis, to build up ring experience again. By beating Mathis early on, Ali would win nothing. A knockout over him would raise little more than an eyebrow, and so the fight found its own level. Ali boxed well within himself, completely unstretched by Mathis, and dictated his own terms. And Mathis, not so dumb as to be unable to take advantage of those opportunities which did arise (or, to be more accurate, those which Ali handed to him on a plate). In the fifth, Ali did little to attack or defend his man: Mathis was able to get close to Ali, and hit him frequently with left and right blows to Ali's head. There was a danger here: if Ali took his opponent too lightly, and relaxed too much, then Mathis might very well land the one punch that was his most effective weapon: a slugging left hook. It was Cooper's left, and Frazier's left, which had sent Ali down before, and Ali's corner, perplexed at the way in which he was fighting this match, urged him not to take things too easily, to lull himself into a false sense of security. Ali's seconds were well aware of the damage to Ali's reputation if Mathis were to bring off an undeserved win, but Ali knew he was in no danger: in the eleventh, a right to Mathis's jaw sent him down, only to see him saved by the bell.

The twelfth round saw Mathis waddle from his corner, and Ali floored him twice in the final round (as he had done in the eleventh), but, in spite of voluble exhortations from his corner to finish Mathis off, he did not bother, and won easily on points.

Why didn't Ali attempt to finish his man off, as he so easily could have done from about the third or fourth rounds onwards? The comments of Ali after his fights have always been very revealing, as well as being almost invariably truthful and objective (if a little over-stated at times). His comments to newspapers declared him to have become a new-found pacifist in the ring, unwilling to cause unnecessary damage to his opponent when he knew he was going to win anyway. Against Ellis, there could well have been extra-ringside considerations for such a humanitarian view, but against Mathis, there was no 'family' connexion. "I wouldn't kill a black man, or a white man, just to give enjoyment to a crowd. It should have been stopped when I started to play around with him in the last round. I'll admit the first ten rounds were dull, but it seems silly to me for two men to stand in a ring and beat each other up."

Many people were perplexed by these remarks. What had happened to Ali? Did the Frazier defeat cause some deep-seated shock which now manifested itself in an unwillingness to defeat lesser fighters in a commanding fashion? Was Ali now wandering gently into some post-championship wilderness? Was this the man who would one day win back the world heavyweight championship? How could he, with this mental outlook?

(3)
December 26th 1971
v JÜRGEN BLIN (WEST GERMANY)
venue: Hallenstadion, Zurich, Switzerland
Muhammad Ali: 15st 12lbs (220lbs)
Jürgen Blin: 14st 2lbs (198lbs)
Referee: Sepp Suter
Attendance: 7,000

Five weeks after cruising to an easy win over Buster Mathis, and five thousand miles away, in Switzerland, Ali fought the heavyweight champion of Germany, Jürgen Blin, in a fight every bit as different from the previous bout as could be wished.

After Ellis and Mathis, Blin appeared to be another candidate for the Aunt Sally road-show, but Ali's shedding of seven pounds and greater concentration on training declared him to be taking this fight rather more seriously than some experts were.

Ali's fourth fight in 1971 was in some ways the best fight he had had that year. Like his counterparts who had fought Ali during the previous twelve months, Blin took the fight to his opponent from the opening bell, caring little for Ali's reputation. This was fine as far as it went, but it was soon obvious that Ali's superior weight and infinitely longer reach would be big hurdles for Blin to overcome.

Blin's only course, as Ellis, Frazier and Bonavena had tried before him, was to attempt to duck and weave under Ali's arms to come to close quarters with him. For a while, this tactic succeeded, but it lay Blin open to danger. The trouble with getting underneath a boxer is that the attack is never delivered from the best position. In a very literal sense, one has to fight one's way upwards and expend energy in getting to something like a good position, which conversely does not allow sufficient space from which to deliver the blows. Apart from anything else, this course of action, unless performed with considerable speed and skill, can be seen coming a mile off, and Ali had been up against enough boxers who had tried this method before to know precisely what to do. As Blin bobbed and ducked his way forward, Ali gradually picked him off with a persistent left jab that always kept Blin at bay. Although Ali's more than adequate defence in this instance prevented Blin from realising to the full his objective, it also meant that Ali was never in a good position from which to deliver any kind of dominant punch. Indeed, for the first three or four rounds, Blin appeared to be making much more of a fight of it than many people would have predicted, and his guts and determination made it far from an easy task for Ali. In the third, as Ali tried to cut loose on his man, Blin refused to be swayed by the sudden outburst, and stood his ground, trading punch for punch in an exchange of quite classic style. For the fourth round, Ali changed his method to one based upon speed, and those observers who felt his legs were suspect in earlier bouts were completely routed. Here was the Ali of old, dancing at incredible speed, jabbing and letting fly with deadly accurate punches to the head, cutting Blin around his left eye, grazing his nose, and badly bruising his right cheek, below and away from his right eye.

At the end of the fourth, it was clear that Blin had been severely mauled, and in the fifth Ali again turned on an exhibition of speed boxing with punch after punch catching Blin full in the face. The German reeled, sent dizzy by Ali's maelstrom of lightning blows, and Blin stumbled back on his heels. Unless Ali had decided that this bout would go the distance, it appeared, as Blin shuffled haplessly back to his corner, that Ali would finish the fight as and when he chose.

The sixth round showed that the exertion of the two previous rounds had in turn taken a little from Ali: he relaxed somewhat, free-wheeling a little, without engaging Blin, who, glad of this respite, tried to attack Ali, but with little success. It was clear that the fight was Ali's, and no way was he going to let the German through to land his favourite combination punches: a right followed by a left hook.

Having rested, so to speak, in the sixth, Ali opened the seventh in killer style. His left arm was ceaseless in action, and more powerful in strength, as it landed again and again on the outboxed German's face and body. Several old-fashioned one-two's from Ali dispatched Blin to the ropes, and as he rebounded into Ali's path the American caught Blin with a deadly accurate left hook which drew the curtains on the German boxer. He fell, not flat out, but to his knees, and tried gamely to beat the count, but failed.

(4)
April 1st 1972
v MAC FOSTER (USA)
venue: Budhokan Hall, Tokyo
Muhammad Ali: 16st 2lbs (226lbs)
Mac Foster: 15st 1¾lbs (211¾lbs)
Referee: John Coreder
Attendance: 15,000

Ali's last win, over Jürgen Blin in Switzerland, had been a highly convincing demonstration of his undimmed powers. Curiously enough his next opponent, Mac Foster, had appeared on the same programme in Zurich, in a good win over the former Italian champion, Bepi Ros, in the eighth round. This was Foster's 29th win in 30 fights — an impressive record, and one of which Ali took due notice when they met in Japan a little over three months later.

November 15th 1962 In round 1, Cassius Clay lands a right to the side of Archie Moore's head

June 18th 1963 At Wembley Stadium, London, at their first meeting, the British and Empire Heavyweight Champion Henry Cooper attacks fiercely in round 1, hoping to land his legendary left hook

In round five, the end is near: a bloody and badly damaged Henry Cooper, his face and body streaked with blood, is retired by referee Little

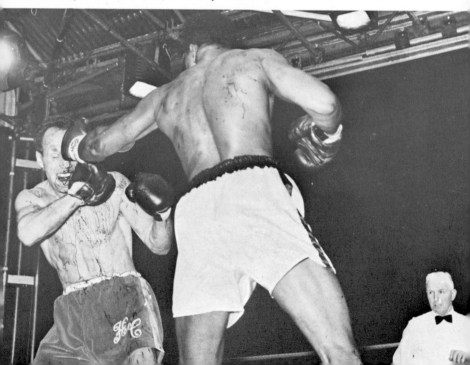

In round four, Cooper succeeds: catching Clay unawares, he floors him, but the ropes and the bell intervene

February 25 1964 In the sixth and last round of his first fight with World Heavyweight Champion Sonny Liston, Cassius Clay lands a left to the champion's right eye

Later in the same round, Clay makes Liston double up from a powerful right to the body. Liston retires at the end of this round and Clay is the new World Heavyweight Champion

May 25th 1965 Less than two minutes into round 1 of their rematch, and Liston is flat on his back, counted out by referee and ex-champion, Jersey Joe Walcott, as Ali glowers over him menacingly

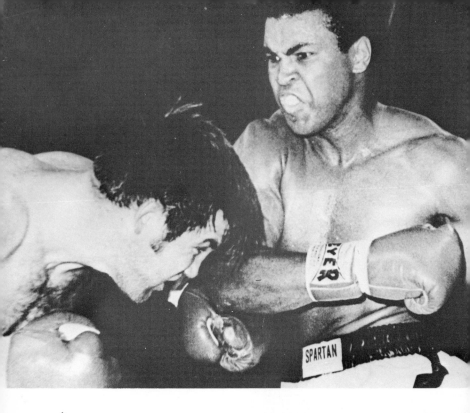

▲
October 26th 1970 After over 3½ years
away from the ring, Muhammad Ali
scores a tremendous victory in his come-
back fight over Jerry Quarry. A right from
Ali catches Quarry in round 3, the round in
which the fight was stopped to save Quarry
from further punishment

The end of the third: Muhammad Ali
congratulated by Bundini Brown after
referee Tony Perez called a halt ▶

March 8th 1971 Joe Frazier, the recognized World Heavyweight Champion, connects solidly to Ali's face in their first meeting. Frazier beat Ali, making Ali's first professional defeat

February 14th 1973 Joe Bugner, the British and European Heavyweight Champion, evades a left from Ali during round 4 of their first fight

March 31st 1973 In round four of the first fight against Ken Norton, his jaw already broken in round 1, Ali aims a right at the ducking Norton's head. Ali lost this fight

September 9th 1973 Recovered from the broken jaw, the rematch with Norton shows a powerful Ali left connecting to Norton's jaw

Later in the same fight, a close-quarter action shot. Ali won the rematch

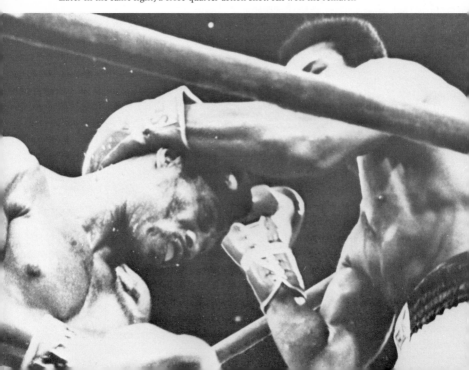

October 30th 1974 In Zaire, against George Foreman, Ali lands a right to Foreman's head. On winning this fight, Ali becomes World Heavyweight Champion for the second time

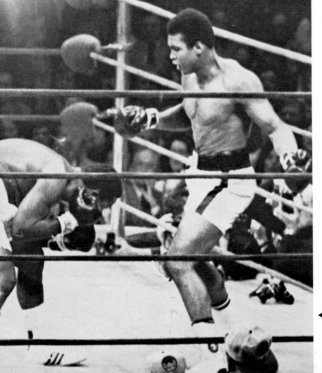

January 28th 1974 The long-awaited rematch with Joe Frazier. In round 1, Frazier ducks below Ali's intended left

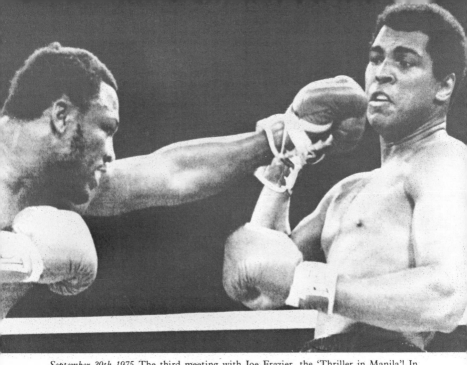

September 30th 1975 The third meeting with Joe Frazier, the 'Thriller in Manila'! In round 1, Joe Frazier lunges with a left to Ali's jaw, but the champion evades the blow

In round 7, Ali glances a right off Frazier's head.

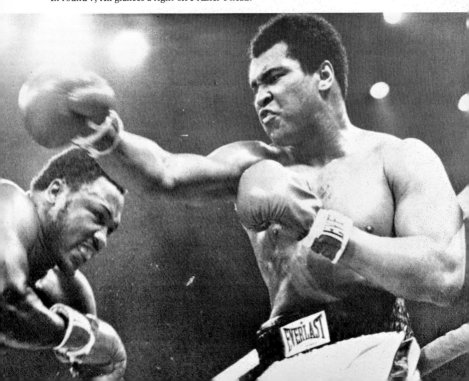

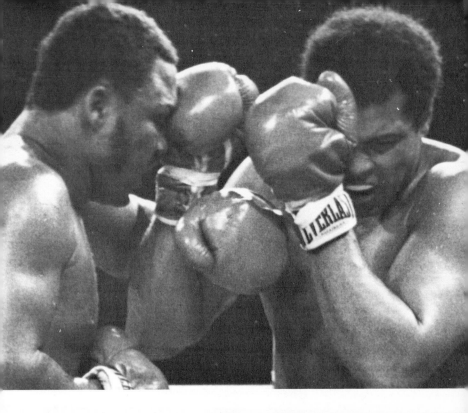

▲
Round 12, as Frazier attempts to engage in close quarter fighting, Ali covers up defensively.

The end is not far away, as in round 13 Ali's left catches Frazier and bends him double, gasping and flat-footed ▶

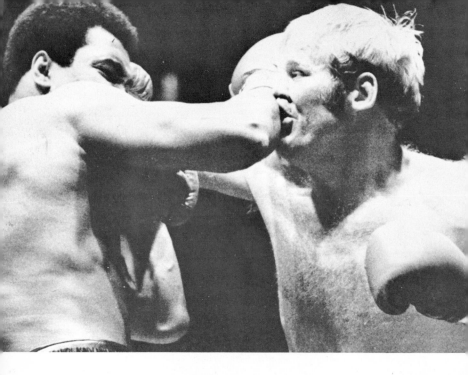

May 25 1976 In round 1 against Richard Dunn of Great Britain, fought in Munich, both boxers connect

By round 5, Ali's power has overcome Dunn's courage. Floored for the fifth time, Dunn rises to his feet to pursue Ali but the referee reckoned Dunn had taken enough punishment ▶

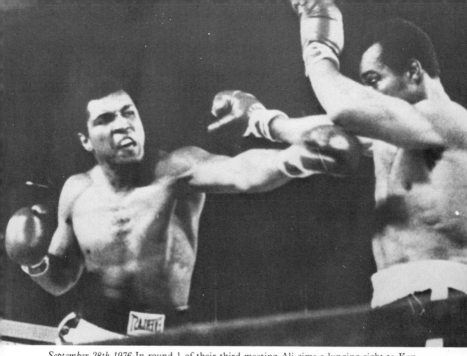

September 28th 1976 In round 1 of their third meeting Ali aims a lunging right to Ken Norton

Several rounds later, and Ali's left connects to Norton's jaw

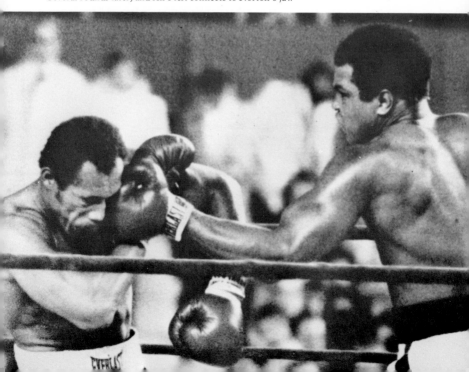

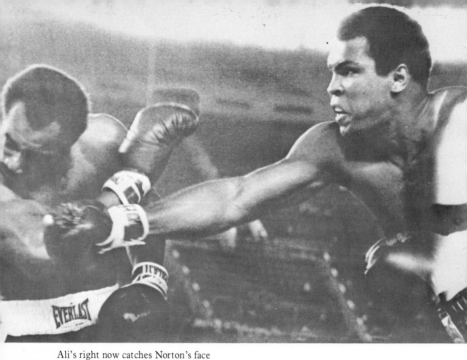

Ali's right now catches Norton's face

February 15th 1978 In round 3 of their first fight in the Las Vegas Hilton Pavilion, the challenger, Leon Spinks, breaks through Ali's guard and connects a right cross to the jaw. Spinks defeats Ali and is the World Heavyweight Champion

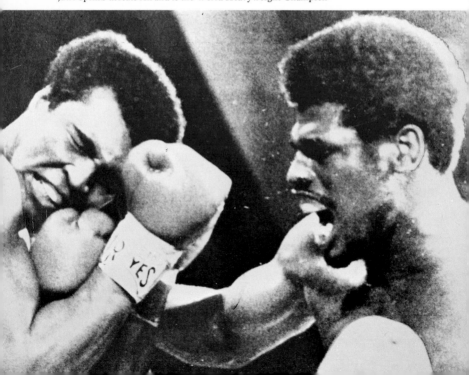

The Tokyo fight was the first professional heavyweight bout ever held in Japan, and the capacity crowd saw a truly remarkable fight. In it, Ali proved his continuing superiority, but his mental approach seemed similar to that which he had shown against Buster Mathis. It appeared that Ali could very well have finished the fight much earlier than he did, but whether it was through indifference, or a desire to give the crowd their money's worth in ring-time (though hardly in persistent boxing action) or, as I suspect, a desire to fight a bout where he could score a convincing win while still boxing well within himself, remained unanswered. Ali still had his eyes and heart fixed on Joe Frazier, and had a hefty series of opponents to meet during 1972 before having a further crack at the title, so it made sense in the long run not to take any undue risks. The Mac Foster fight, therefore, hardly qualifies as one of Ali's greatest, but it still contains pointers to the chameleon-like fighting nature of this extraordinary boxer.

Unlike his previous opponents, Ali found Foster an easy target in the first round: Foster was in superb physical condition, but he lacked the speed necessary to get underneath Ali's reach. The first round, therefore, went well for Ali, who was in no trouble at all. The second showed a sudden change of pace: this time from Foster, who surprised Ali on one or two occasions with powerful scoring punches to the body and some long, arching head shots. Foster had evened up the fight, and it was on the cards that this could develop into a truly classic encounter. In the third, it was Ali who again took the initiative, relying on his clear jabbing and superior speed to pick off Foster, keeping his opponent at bay with his superior reach and elegant footwork. In the fourth, the bout began to go the way of all flesh as Ali kept up this relentless worrying, landing some powerful bombs that certainly shook Foster. Ali had predicted he would win in the fifth, but Foster was proving more of a handful than such a win would have indicated, and possibly Ali left his attack in the fourth a little too late before delivering the quietus in the fifth. Ali came out for the fifth eagerly, anxious to make his prediction come true, but Foster was a match for him: he managed to fend off Ali's attacks in the fifth, and even though Ali landed some telling blows to Foster's head and body, they were not cleanly struck, nor were they powerful enough to stop him. After the exertions in the fifth, Ali slowed the pace right down, being content, knowing that psychologically the fight was his, to score with his superior ringcraft and pile up an unassailable lead on points. Ali appeared at times to be toying with Foster, groping around his neck like a crazy parody of himself, and he took this threat with such apparent ease that Foster won the seventh, and Ali did nothing to score. Ali was so far ahead that nothing could catch him. In the later rounds, the ninth, eleventh and last two rounds, Ali gently turned on the fuel, dominating his opponent and shaking him with sudden bursts of speed and accurate, heavy punches. Foster was gradually reduced to a humble level, which made nonsense of his previous excellent record, and when the final bell came, he looked genuinely relieved. This was not so much because of the state to which Ali had fought him, but also because none of Foster's previous fights had lasted past the eighth round. Foster might well have found himself lacking the stamina which a fifteen-round fight demands. Ali certainly proved that he possessed it in full, and, in so doing, once again humbled a worthy opponent in a totally commanding and almost perfunctory manner. Within a month Ali would be fighting again, halfway round the world. He really was in an extraordinary situation, still nagging away at Frazier's shoulder.

(5)
May 1st 1972
v GEORGE CHUVALO (CANADA)
venue: Vancouver
Muhammad Ali: 15st 7½lbs (217½lbs)
George Chuvalo: 15st 11lbs (221lbs)
Referee: Dave Brown
Attendance: 8,000

A little over six years before, the Canadian heavyweight champion George Chuvalo had forced Ali, for the first time in his professional career, to go the full distance. In the end, of course, Ali had prevailed, but it had been a much tougher fight than many had predicted. Now that Ali was back in the ring, and getting a number of fights under his belt before he tried to wrest the crown from Joe Frazier, it was natural, as Chuvalo was still fighting professionally, and fighting well, there should be a rematch. More than normal interest centred on this fight: this was the first time a boxer who had fought Ali before his exile was scheduled to fight him since his comeback. As Ali's style had changed noticeably since his return, and as Chuvalo had given him a sizeable run for his money before — and as Ali had been shown to be vulnerable — then the interest surrounding this particular bout can well be appreciated. The bout took place in Chuvalo's native Canada, as before, but this time on the other side of the country, in Vancouver.

Chuvalo, then thirty-four, had been decisively beaten by George Foreman in 1970. He lacked the speed of his youth, but the same was true of Ali, who was now thirty. Few would have believed it had they not known, for from the start Ali danced around the ring as of old, as if to show that the years had not dimmed his physical activity. It really was a curious sight: in previous fights during the year, we have seen how at times Ali appeared tired, occasionally disinterested, clearly lacking the incessant energy of his pre-exile days. Yet here, against Chuvalo, his fifth fight in just over ten months, he had recaptured his old pace. As if to prove his detractors wrong, Ali again showed another facet of his complex character.

The demonstration, however, was at Chuvalo's expense: the Canadian had been well briefed concerning those opponents of Ali who had found a way past his deadly left jabs. Chuvalo came forward incessantly, but this time Ali's speed was always too great for Chuvalo, who, in trying to trap Ali against the ropes, frequently found himself wrong-footed or totally bemused as his powerful punches landed on thin air. All this happened in spite of Ali's somewhat dangerous ploy of appearing to allow himself to be trapped on the ropes, challenging Chuvalo to attack him. Chuvalo, however, had not fought Ali before for nothing: this time, in a moment of delicious table-turning, it was Chuvalo who refused to take up the bait, and stood his ground, ignoring Ali on the ropes and in turn waiting for Ali to come after him. Many appreciated Chuvalo's surprising action, but this was a mere foretaste of what was to come when, in the seventh round, it was Chuvalo who showed what he had learned from Ali by lowering his hands, and daring Ali to hit him. Ali must have been bemused in having the tables so effectively turned on him, and there could have been a touch of needle in Chuvalo's attitude, for he had not been hit hard enough to floor him in either bout. By challenging Ali, Chuvalo appeared to humiliate the American: it was a remarkable turn of events, and Ali took up this challenge, and hit Chuvalo repeatedly with more venom and impetus than before, opening up a cut on Chuvalo's mouth. It says much for the Canadian's strength that, even though Ali had built up a big points lead, it was Chuvalo's challenge that spurred Ali on to make the only attack which drew blood.

Still Chuvalo came forward, surely knowing he was far behind on points, hoping to catch the elusive Ali with a left hook, but to no avail: Ali's combination punches, his jabs and hooks, crosses and uppercuts — all would have severely damaged a less tough and invincible fighter. Ali hurt Chuvalo, who swayed several times, but still, as in their first fight, he refused to go down. In the final round Ali attacked again at will, with greater ferocity than he had shown against Foster, Mathis or even Jimmy Ellis, determined to fell Chuvalo, but for all the fury and accuracy, he failed. Chuvalo even shouted "That wasn't much of a punch", to Ali, but he told a different story after the fight. The bell brought the match to an end, and Ali was a unanimous winner on points. Chuvalo, a worthy opponent, had been outboxed by superior skill.

Ali had won again, and won well, but his power did seem suspect, if he was to regain his title from Frazier. Chuvalo, however, said later that Ali was in much better shape than he thought he would be (the reports of Ali's supposedly poor showings had misled him), and even better than he had been six years before. Although some will think that Chuvalo's comments were little more than excuses for his own failure, Ali was undoubtedly sharper than Chuvalo was led to believe, and he was without question a vastly more experienced boxer than on their first

77

meeting. Ali was still a formidable opponent, and he still stalked Frazier.

(6)
June 27th 1972
v JERRY QUARRY (USA)
venue: Las Vegas Convention Center
Muhammad Ali: 15st 6½lbs (216½lbs)
Jerry Quarry: 14st 2lbs (198lbs)
Referee: Mike Kaplan
Attendance: unrecorded

It will be remembered that Jerry Quarry was Ali's first opponent since his return to the professional ring, at Atlanta, Georgia, on October 26th 1970. Ali's victory over Quarry was complete and utterly devastating, but during the intervening twenty months seven other fights had not always lived up to the expectations of the first Quarry bout. Quarry, too, having seen the way Ali's career had twisted and turned since then probably thought he stood a better chance against Ali than at first, and so he eagerly accepted the chance of a rematch. If he had heard the reports of Ali's previous fights, he might well have been misled by some of them: the boxing press had not enthused over Ali's wins against Ellis, Mathis, Blin or Mac Foster, nor had they been carried away by the defeat of Chuvalo, but it was Chuvalo's comment after that fight to which Quarry should have paid more attention.

The first two rounds were evenly matched: Ali began as before, a combination of moving in at speed, dancing around his opponent, and scoring with those softening left jabs. He had no real need to size Quarry up as they had met before, but the same was true of Quarry's side: there is no substitute for experience, and Quarry knew Ali a lot better than when they first met. He countered several of Ali's punches, but by the third round it became clear he was having difficulty in getting past Ali, inside the legendary left hook. Quarry managed to land a few hefty blows to the body, but Ali's sharpness and accuracy in hitting Quarry's head almost incessantly meant that unless Quarry was able to mount a considerable change of style and approach, then Ali could walk away with this fight as commandingly as he had done on their first meeting.

In the fifth and sixth, Ali drew far ahead on points. Quarry, for all his solid qualities and doubtless courage, was clearly outclassed, and it was purely the changed demands on Ali at this fight which enabled the bout to go on for a longer distance than at their first meeting.

For his come-back in 1970, Ali knew a tremendous amount was at stake. He had to show that nothing had changed, that he was still the most dangerous and charismatic boxer in the world, and a win over

Quarry had to be a crushing one, positively blitzkrieg-like in its fury and deadliness. But on this occasion, the pressures on Ali were not so great: he did not have to prove himself quite so much as in 1970.

Quarry charged at Ali, slugging and throwing brawny hooks at him, but for each one that landed, twenty missed, as Ali side-stepped, picking off Quarry as he did so with full-blooded combination punches. In the seventh he caught him with an adamantine blow and Quarry fell. He was counted out.

The tiredness which people had begun to notice in Ali's earlier fights was admitted by him after this second Quarry fight. Ali said he was surprised at his own speed and stamina, and he would tire much quicker than he did, adding that "I am stronger and more experienced than I have been in my whole life."

(7)
July 19th 1972
v AL 'BLUE' LEWIS (USA)
venue: Croke Park, Dublin
Muhammad Ali: 15st 7½lbs (217½lbs)
Al 'Blue' Lewis: 15st 13½lbs (223½lbs)
Referee: Lew Eskin
Attendance: 20,000

With this fight in Eire, Ali fought his fifth consecutive fight in a different country. In eight months he had fought in Switzerland, Japan, Canada, the USA, and now Eire — a much more international and 'world-champion-like' succession of matches than Joe Frazier was undertaking. But no matter how well he felt in himself, Ali's incessant travelling and constant preparation and fighting were beginning to take their toll.

Three days before the fight, Ali caught cold, but it was not sufficient to stop him, nor to prevent him scoring yet another very good win over his fellow-American from Detroit. In fact, the opening round was so good for Ali that this bout, the first world heavyweight fight in Ireland for 64 years, might well have ended in the first few minutes as a quick opening left Ali with a perfect target at which to aim a doughty left hook. It caught Lewis severely, and sent him reeling on his heels, shocked almost senseless by the punch. Miraculously, Lewis managed to shake off the effects of the blow, and came battling back to Ali, but already, as the bell went, it appeared that blood was trickling from Lewis's mouth. Ali needed no second telling that he had already delivered what could have been the blow to end the fight, for he came out at the start of the second like a tiger, suddenly released from his cage. Time and time again, Ali sank mighty lefts into Lewis's body, winding him, and causing him to stagger, as a ship buffeted by furious waves in a gathering storm. Ali almost crouched in this round, as if to pounce on his man, but Lewis was far from finished. The third round started again with all-action from Ali, as he caught Lewis repeatedly with combination punches once more to the body. Lewis staggered again, uncertain as to the impetus of the fight, but, drawing on a deep reserve of strength, it was Lewis who managed to launch a counter-attack, as Ali slightly let-up after his ferocious affray. The crowd urged their approval of Lewis's courage, and it was clear he was not giving up without a fight. Ali sensed this, and in the fourth he launched a stunning attack: this was the Ali of old, out to get his man, the killer instinct returned, totally refuting those charges of half-heartedness that has been bandied about before. Ali connected many times with husky left jabs to Lewis's face, and again attacked his body with deadly accuracy and power. The power of Ali's punches seemed to grow with kinetic energy as each one landed, for towards the end of the round he caught Lewis with the most impacted punch of the fight, straight to Lewis's head, which kicked back as if struck full across the face with a piece of wood. The bell intervened, and Lewis returned to the calm of his corner seat.

Again, in the fifth, Ali seemed determined to end it once and for all, as he never let up his fierce attack. Lewis's courage was quite remarkable, as he absorbed many punches which would have finished a lesser man. He still had the fibre to come forward and land blows on Ali's body — a heroic gesture, but not enough. Ali connected yet again with a tremendous left hook which sent Lewis flying backwards on his feet and flat on his back. The American referee, Lew Eskin, the executive editor and associate publisher of *Boxing Illustrated*, counted to nine, although some thought he could have counted to twelve in the time, and Lewis managed, with great courage, to stagger to his feet. Eskin was obliged to wipe Lewis's gloves, and while doing this, the bell signalled the end of the round. Ali's chance, which he had every reason to think he had taken well, and won well, had gone, and Lewis had escaped again.

Another question mark has to be raised over the standard of the refereeing during the sixth round, for the tape binding Ali's left glove had worked loose. As the round progressed, a trailing piece of bandage got longer, until it measured about twelve inches and was flapping disconcertingly and possibly dangerously — to both boxers. The referee did not attend to this at all during the round, apparently unconcerned as it got worse, quite oblivious to the rules of the ring, the danger to the fighters, or the cries from the ringside. It is not surprising, therefore, that the sixth round marked a distinct lowering of action and temperature, and Ali appeared disconcerted at the way things had gone. In the seventh it was Lewis who began to fight back, and managed to hit Ali straight on the nose, which drew blood down across Ali's face. In the eighth, too, Ali seemed muted compared to his earlier energy, allowing Lewis to get through with a strapping combination of lefts and rights to the head. There was growing power behind these punches, and Ali surely felt them.

But Ali had back-pedalled enough: in the ninth he came out as at the start of round two, unwilling to lose the advantage he had so massively built up at the start of the fight. A whole succession of punches to Lewis's head caught him off guard, but there was more fury in them than accuracy, for rather too many missed for comfort. Lewis was again able to mount a counter-attack, his fire roused by his comparative successes in the middle rounds. In the tenth, however, it was clear that Lewis's strength was flowing away from him, with Ali returning to his insistent jabbing and weaving, as though it was round three, and not seven rounds later. Even Mr Eskin realised it was all over in the eleventh, as just into the second minute of the round he stopped the fight.

Lewis had done much to earn the respect and admiration of the crowd in absorbing a frightening succession of Ali's best punches, and still finding the strength of character to come forward, but Ali's win was as total and icily cool as could be. Lewis had had a few lucky let-offs, which affected Ali's composure, as did the scene after the fight was over, when the ring became packed with people and intermittent fighting broke out. This was an unworthy end to a fascinating fight, one which was much better and much more interesting than some would have us believe.

(8)
September 20th 1972
v FLOYD PATTERSON (USA)
venue: Madison Square Garden, New York City
Muhammad Ali: 15st 8lbs (218lbs)
Floyd Patterson: 13st 6½lbs (188½lbs)
Referee: Arthur Mercante
Attendance: 17,348

Floyd Patterson, thirty-seven at the time of his second meeting with Ali, was one of the best liked and most respected heavyweight fighters in his day. A vastly experienced man, Patterson had done something which no other fighter had ever achieved, and which Ali was striving to emulate: he had won the world heavyweight title twice, but at thirty-seven, many felt that he was way past his best, and would be a much easier opponent for Ali than he had been seven years before.

There appears little doubt that Ali believed this, too, for quite apart from the age difference there was a tremendous weight difference. It almost did not quite work out that way, for in the opening rounds Patterson fought almost beyond belief. The fifth man to fight Ali twice, Patterson's immense skill came close to overwhelming Ali early on, who seemed at times totally perplexed at the 'old man's' agility. Patterson more than matched Ali for speed, and came at Ali from under his swings to attack him consistently, and with conspicuous success. It was obvious as the early rounds of the fight progressed that Ali was in some danger. If the first two rounds were even, Ali clearly lost the next three as Patterson was able to land, score and hurt with his finely-tuned and superbly-judged punches. For many moments, it seemed as though Ali had taken this fight far too lightly, and his training for it was not as sharp nor as dedicated as it ought to have been. Joe Frazier was in the audience, and before the fight began was introduced to the audience from the ring. Ali put on a show of wanting to get at him then and there, but Frazier must have felt secure at any future meeting with Ali on the showing of this fight with Patterson.

Patterson's defence, too, could have taught Ali a thing or two. Ali found it increasingly difficult to get through it, and land any punch worth recalling, and it transpired that Ali would have to pull out a few more stops if he was going to win. In the sixth came the expected, and overdue, Ali onslaught: faster, more determined than at any time in the fight, Ali let fly with a sustained combination attack to Patterson's face, which opened a nasty cut above Patterson's left eye. Three right crosses caught Patterson's jaw in succession and for the first time the older man was in trouble, bad trouble.

The bell intervened, and Ali came out for the seventh more determined than ever. He attacked Patterson's temporarily-patched cut, which soon opened again, with blood oozing freely from the dangerous wound. With Patterson back on the defensive, unable to see clearly, and naturally in difficulty, Ali attacked his man again. He caught him to the body and again on the jaw, and again Patterson was frustrated and hindered, looking old and damaged. By the end of the round, his eye was in an awful condition, and the official doctor of the New York Boxing Commission, on hand at the ringside, ordered the referee to stop the fight. Patterson bowed to the opinion of the doctor, and did not rise from his seat when the bell went for the start of the eighth, but afterwards, when Patterson had recovered, Ali complimented him, saying: "He fought a great fight. He shook me twice. He was harder to hit than in our first fight and I think he is entitled to a rematch." As if to scotch any rumours as to the nature and quality of the fight, Patterson himself added: "I hope you saw it as I saw it. Ali didn't carry me and I was holding my own when the fight was stopped."

There was no comment from Joe Frazier.

(9)
November 21st 1972
v BOB FOSTER (USA)
venue: Sahara Tahoe Hotel, Stateline, Nevada
Muhammad Ali: 15st 11¼lbs (221¼lbs)
Bob Foster: 12st 12lbs (180lbs)
Referee: Mills Lane
Attendance: 2,000 (Dinner Club)

In some professions, there are always convincing reasons to take a 'second-string' engagement from time to time, even if it is done for the most mundane of all reasons — money. A concert pianist, for example, might like to 'play-in' an unfamiliar concerto with an unranked orchestra, to iron out any rough edges in almost a public practice, before playing the same piece with a world-class symphony orchestra before a highly critical audience.

For a boxer, however, there would at first sight appear to be no reasons — apart from financial ones — to accept a match against a fighter who seems to have no chance at all against him. Such a fighter against Muhammad Ali was Bob Foster, 41lbs lighter than Ali. The difference in weight almost literally made the fight one-sided, but if there is anything certain in the fight game, it is that it is uncertain. However lowly Bob Foster might have seemed to the connoisseurs of boxing before he got in that ring, he achieved something which greater fighters than he had failed to do.

The first two rounds told us little: Ali probed and jabbed in his classic style, Foster able to do little to counter the rapidly-scoring and deadly-accurate volleys. By the third round Ali had completely summed up his opponent, and started a routine which had been absent from his repertoire for some time. He patted Foster gently, in mock sympathy, and pretended to be hurt by the far-from-dangerous punches of his opponent. Those to whom such action is reprehensible forget that Ali had used it before to great effect — not just on his audience but on his opponent — for the psychological damage can be worth landing a multitude of punches on the losing boxer. It opened up Ali's defences in a way that, unless judged to perfection, would be foolhardy in the extreme. Ali was in no danger, it appeared, for he had already built up a commanding lead on points. He continued his attacks with increasing power in the fourth, and in the fifth — the round he predicted the fight would end in — he really went after his man. Foster was stunned by the barrage, and he went down. Up again a few moments later, he was again on the floor from a powerful combination. A third, and even a fourth time, and Foster was sent to the canvas. Under New York law, Ali would have already won (with three knock-downs in one round), but in Nevada, which sets its own standards for most things, he had to be winner only by flooring his opponent for a complete count. Foster staggered up after the fourth knock-down, and it looked to be curtains for him.

However, two strange things occurred in the fifth. The first was that Ali's efforts had tired him almost as much as Foster, and, not for the first time in his career, Ali relaxed the pace considerably in the next round, taking a breather. The other thing, which may have had some bearing on Ali's demeanour, was that Foster, in one of his few hitting changes in the fifth, actually caught Ali a nasty blow to the head cutting him under the left eyebrow. This was far and away the most serious facial injury Ali had sustained in his professional career, and, by one of those quirks of circumstance, it was achieved by his lightest opponent.

In the seventh, his eye repaired, Ali resumed the attack, and floored Foster twice. Foster however, no doubt encouraged by cutting Ali, managed to hit Ali squarely several times, and Ali, exaggerating Foster's effectiveness, staggered around the ring, clowning by pretending to sag at the knees. Foster was finished — forty seconds into the eighth round Ali landed a blow from a snaking long right hand which catapulted Foster to the floor for the seventh and last time.

Ali's cut was no light affair — it needed five stitches, so Foster, in spite of his overwhelming defeat, had given Ali something to remember him by. Foster came in for a fair amount of adverse comment from the fight press, but before this bout he had managed a highly creditable 42 knockouts in his 54 professional fights. He did not lack the experience, but, as he admitted later, he lacked the weight. To have gone down six times for counts of eight against Ali before finally being knocked out, *and* to have cut Ali badly, showed that whatever complaint might be levelled at Foster, he was no coward.

The question that remained was why Ali needed to fight Foster at all. He had already had five fights that year, and the Foster meeting meant eight bouts in one year and four days. From these Ali had earned over two million dollars so his $260,000 purse from the Foster meeting — although easy pickings — was hardly an over-riding consideration. The real reasons could be more deep-seated and less superficially obvious. Ali's defeat at Frazier's hands, although taken like a gentleman, still rankled. He wanted, more than anything else, to beat Frazier, and he knew that one way to get himself ready for that day was to keep himself at it. Frazier, by contrast, had defended his title much less frequently than Ali had done, and was far less active as a boxer than Ali. Ali's continuous activity, not always against the best opposition, also kept his name before the public, and Ali was a past master at the use of publicity.

Frazier, in his title defences, had been matched sometimes against fighters of quite mediocre standards, so even if some of Ali's opponents appeared outclassed, Ali was not alone. The fact remains that at the time, there were not enough world-class heavyweights able or willing to sustain a regular series of top-notch fights for Frazier or Ali. Indeed, and this is a crucial point to remember, out of the top dozen heavyweights in the world at that time, Ali had met and beaten eight of them — not including Bob Foster, the leading world light heavyweight contender — within the previous two years. Against this background, the 'unsuitability' of Ali's opponents, bandied about by people who ought to know better, appears pointless and carping criticism. Ali ducked nobody.

(10)
February 14th 1973
v JOE BUGNER (GREAT BRITAIN)
venue: Convention Centre, Las Vegas
Muhammad Ali: 15st 7½lbs (217½lbs)
Joe Bugner: 15st 9 lbs (219lbs)
Referee: Buddy Basilico
Attendance: 5,700

In the three months between the Bob Foster fight and the first fight against Joe Bugner, the boxing world was shaken by an event which took place on January 22nd, 1973. Joe Frazier, the heavyweight champion of the world, came up against George Foreman (who was also an Olympic medallist from 1968). They fought in Kingston, Jamaica, or rather the bout took place there, for few people who saw Frazier score his classic victory over Ali could recognise him as the same man who was unceremoniously beaten by George Foreman after the referee stopped the fight, one minute thirty seconds into round two. Foreman had knocked Frazier down six times in the fight, to win the world heavyweight crown. Ali now had two men to beat.

Ali knew the days of less-than-total commitment were over: his contract to fight Bugner had raised a few eyebrows, but in fact Bugner only accepted on the third occasion. Bugner, whose family had fled to England in 1956 from Hungary at the time of the uprising, was a fighter for whom Ali had great respect. Bugner had trained with Ali and sparred with him, and had defeated Henry Cooper in a controversial decision some time before. Bugner was nine years younger than Ali, and at twenty-two was a veteran of 49 professional fights (7 more than Ali), So for his age he was an immensely experienced boxer. Ali had predicted that one day Bugner would become world heavyweight champion. This view was not shared by all fight fans, who regarded this claim by Ali as an attempt to class-up the opposition. Bugner lacked nothing in experience, although he had given some lack-lustre perform-ances, and, unlike Ali's two previous opponents, he was giving nothing away in the matter of weight. His style, marked by a dogged persistence, could have proved dangerous to Ali, if the fight was to go the full distance.

Round one began with both boxers sizing up each other: it was clear that Ali did not treat Bugner as a piece of cake. He soon began his traditional attack of jabbing and weaving. One way around Ali's persistent motion was to stay near the ropes, and this is what Bugner did. However, this in turn brings its own dangers: in the first round, Bugner paid the price for his too-cautious approach when Ali caught him with a searing left hook just under his left eye, which swelled greatly. Although blood did not flow, the round was Ali's, and he had stamped his personality on the fight forcibly.

Bugner was clearly off-key in round two, although he landed several times to Ali's head and body. He was forced back again on the defensive as Ali counter-attacked, aiming for Bugner's suspect left eye, which began to bleed heavily. It says much for Bugner's defensive position that Ali was unable to finish him off at this time, and in spite of a prolonged attack in the third, Bugner still hung on grimly, refusing to acknowledge defeat. Encouraged by having weathered the opening storm, Bugner came out at the start of the fourth with marked purpose, intending to force Ali back and to take the fight to him. Ali's cat-like ringcraft enabled him to use the ropes to his own advantage, throwing himself back and away from Bugner's fists. Ali continued to evade Bugner in the fifth, but the Britisher's left hooks and crosses only just missed Ali's head. Round six started as though this was the one in which Ali would finish it, for he tore into Bugner with a fierce determination that was fearful to behold. Bugner took a tremendous amount of punishment from Ali, but doggedly refused to go down, and even managed a few counter-attacks, although they were as nothing compared to Ali's fire-power. Bugner still had a lot of fight left in him, and in the seventh, the round in which Ali took his by-now usual breather, it was Bugner who moved to the attack, scoring and hurting the American, and in the eighth it was Bugner again who seemed to be reviving himself and taking the fight to Ali by catching him with a powerful right cross straight on Ali's jaw. For a few seconds, it was all-Bugner, as Ali tried to see a way through the British man's log-like defence. The way through was the way in which Ali had begun the fight: in the following round, instead of meeting Bugner face-on, Ali began to dance round again and again, as he weighed up the opponent, trying to glimpse the opening for his shots. It was Bugner, however, who caught Ali with two successive rights to the head which, as Ali confessed later, "made me hear bells". But this attack only served to spur Ali again to a ferocious outburst, and in round ten Ali attacked the vulnerable eye. This time it broke open, like a cracked dam, and blood spilled down over Bugner's face, as Ali, seizing the opportunity he had so cleverly made for himself, proceeded to do great damage to Bugner's face. At the end of round ten, blood poured over Bugner's nose and jaws from two cuts, like the Tigris and the Euphrates meeting in the Persian Gulf of Bugner's chin.

Bugner's corner performed miracles during the interval, for when the eleventh started it looked as though the temporary medication had done the trick. It was too much to hope for: Ali again caught the wounds with vicious hooks and the blood ran again. Gamely Bugner held on, in both senses, and at the start of the final round attempted to throw all his strength behind a series of blows at Ali which, if they had connected properly, might have pulled off the surprise. It was not to be: although Bugner refused to go down, Ali persistently attacked him, increasing the damage to Bugner's eyes, so that, at the end, Bugner's face paid the penalty for a style of attack which relied too much on ring positioning to pin his man down, rather than the moving and weaving under Ali's flying arms which several boxers had found so successful in the past.

And so Ali won on points — a clear winner, and in retrospect an easy winner, but Bugner was still a very young man, and had been the first British boxer to go the full distance with Ali — something which only five boxers had ever done before. He had certainly lived to fight another day.

(11)
March 31st 1973
v KEN NORTON (USA)
venue: San Diego Sports Arena
Muhammad Ali: 15st 11lbs (221lbs)
Ken Norton: 15st 0lbs (210lbs)
Referee: Frank Rustich
Attendance: 12,000

This far, Ali's progress towards regaining the world championship was proceeding well. His wins over the previous two years had been more than good enough to show that he had the will and the ability to realise his goal. George Foreman's win over Joe Frazier had added a new dimension to his task, for Ali had not fought Foreman, and in many ways Foreman was an unknown figure. For the time being, Frazier remained Ali's prime target, and after that, if he was still champion, Foreman was next on the shopping list.

Ken Norton, Ali's next opponent, appeared comparatively easy meat in this company. Rated seventh in the world, he had met little opposition of note. His fight with Ali held out the prospect of stardom if he could win, and, aided and abetted by trainer Eddie Futch (Frazier's trainer at the time he defeated Ali), he prepared for the moment of truth. Whether Ali prepared as thoroughly for this fight as he should have will remain an unanswerable question, but there is little doubt that the decision, when it came, caused the biggest jolt to Ali's career that he had ever experienced in the ring.

In the first round, both boxers came out more tentative than aggressive, each sizing up the other, with Norton adopting a far from orthodox approach to Ali, whose speed seemed faintly suspect, no doubt as a result of his continuous fighting over the previous twelve months. Because of this, Ali was forced to box closer to his opponent than he would otherwise have liked, and it was disturbing to see Ali lacking pace at the very beginning of the fight. But how often have we thought one thing about Ali, only to see it flatly contradicted the next moment? Norton continued his attacks, and got through Ali's guard in a dangerous manner. The second round began in the same way, but Ali soon took the initiative. Suddenly, he unleashed a fury of lefts to Norton's head, which shook him badly. The film showed that Ali landed seven consecutive lefts in that attack before Norton could retaliate, and then one of the most remarkable things in Ali's remarkable career occurred. Norton broke Ali's jaw.

Angelo Dundee recalled that the dental treatment Ali underwent prior to the fight, which included the removal of two troublesome back teeth, left Ali's jaw comparatively at risk, and a powerful retaliatory blow by Norton which landed clear on Ali's jaw itself coincided with Ali opening his mouth. At that point the jaw, faintly weakened, was at its most exposed, and it cracked, fracturing badly and causing blood to ooze up in Ali's mouth. When he got back to the corner, Ali asked his seconds to describe the symptoms of a broken jaw. Bundini demonstrated, and Ali knew his jaw was broken. His corner was horrified: to permit a boxer to continue with a broken jaw is to take an appalling risk. Muhammad Ali was always master of his own destiny: he knew he had caught Norton in the second, and with ten further rounds, he had a very good chance of winning the fight earlier, as long as he could keep out of trouble. In addition, Joe Frazier was in the audience. And so the fight continued, with rounds three and four similar in activity. Ali attempted to overcome the immense pain and terrible danger, and land knockout blows on Norton, who was unaware of the damage he had caused inside Ali's head. At the end of the third, blood was flowing out of Ali's mouth, but there was nothing his seconds could do, short of major surgery, to staunch the rivulet.

In the circumstances, it is amazing the fight continued at all, but Norton's rougher, slugging style, coupled with the drain on Ali's mental and physical reserves from his injury, meant that Norton gradually overhauled Ali's slender points lead. Ali, however, was impelled by things which over-ride physical limitations — his indomitable will-power, his utter refusal to admit defeat and his resolve to win back the heavyweight crown — fuelled his body. He found the energy to land powerful lefts and rights to Norton's head and body, putting himself in terrible danger by his close proximity to Norton. In the sixth round, Norton again got through by landing a right to Ali's head which must have resounded like Doomsday in Ali's brain. But still Ali refused to give up — goodness knows what must have gone through his mind, the minds of his seconds, and the minds of the ringside crowd as this great fighter was reduced in stature.

The war of attrition continued, and in the tenth, Norton again got through Ali's guard to land a carbon copy of the blow which had hurt so much in the sixth — Ali was lifted skywards by the velocity, but whether it was from Norton's strength or his own body recoiling instinctively from further pain, or — most likely — a combination of both, is unclear. Whatever caused it, it was Norton's round. It seemed as though nothing could now stop Norton winning a major upset, but in the eleventh, Ali's greatest round without question in this fight, and one of the most heroic rounds he ever fought, he came back at Norton seemingly with his power undimmed, shrugging off his troubles as if discarding an old cloak, and went after Norton, catching him again and again with titanic punches. A combination — a double left hook, delivered at speed and with tremendous force — caught Norton full on the head, and his legs buckled, sagging, as a wave of unconsciousness flitted across his mind. The crowd could not believe it, but Ali just lacked that additional ounce of vim, the last grain of grit, to force Norton down for the count.

The effort was too much: in the last round, Ali appeared as though he had really shot his bolt, with all energy spent. He gamely struggled through the round, his legs wooden and he became a cruel parody of an ageing fighter, reduced to blocking and fending-off as best he could the incessant rain of punches from Norton, whose energy gathered in momentum as he shook off the effects of Ali's earlier attack and realised the fight was within his grasp. As the bell sounded, it was clear that, whichever way it was to go, the decision would be close. Norton got the win on a split decision: it was a fractional win, but it was a win.

Pandemonium broke out: Ali had been beaten by a comparative unknown. Ali was taken to Claremont Hospital in San Diego, where pictures showed the broken jaw had separated by a quarter of an inch. The surgeons found it impossible to believe that Ali had fought a professional heavyweight fight for ten rounds with such an injury, and had, moreover, come within an ace of winning. Ali's wife, Belinda, was also taken to the hospital, suffering from shock.

At first, few could believe that Ali had been so badly injured, almost as though it had been a fabrication to detract from Norton's win. But the pictures of Ali's face, wired up, the medical reports, and the doctor's demands that Ali would be out of the ring for many months, told their own story. Ali's dreams of regaining his title faded into fairyland in the light of this defeat. He was thirty-one, with a severely broken jaw, defeated for the second time — and by an unknown. The mountain he had to climb, made up of Norton, Frazier and Foreman, was so formidable and so high that no-one thought it could ever be done. If that mountain showed no inclination to come to Muhammad, then Muhammad would have to go to the mountain by himself.

CHAPTER TEN

Muhammad Climbs the Mountain

(1)
September 10th 1973
v KEN NORTON (USA)
venue: Los Angeles Inglewood Forum
Muhammad Ali: 15st 2lbs (212lbs)
Ken Norton: 14st 9lbs (205lbs)
Referee: Dick Young
Attendance: 12,100

In the Summer of 1973, Ali's professional career was at its lowest ebb. History tells of many men, in all walks of life, who have achieved a measure of greatness, and yet while in their prime find that what they have achieved has been taken from them. At such moments, the individual's reaction reveals more of his inner character than almost any other situation. The prize, the thing which mattered so much, is gone, and in politics, for example, there have been defeated leaders who have disappeared for ever from public life, unable to face the humiliation, so depleted in energy that a come-back is out of the question. Boxers, as well as other athletes, have — after the great defeat — often faded completely from public view. As Floyd Patterson once so graphically described, the defeat of a great boxer frequently marks the first step back along the road, along the slippery slope which leads to the slums from which he came. Not all men can use the catharsis of defeat to rebuild their lives, by no means anxious to regain that which they have lost. If properly used, a period of rebuilding — hopefully avoiding the mistakes which led to the loss — can add further dimensions to the character of the individual. Human relationships frequently change, as no-one wants to know the loser. It is during such circumstances that essential truths reveal themselves in many ways: one certainly discovers who one's true friends are, and what one's real objectives in life are. One discovers what are the really valuable things, and if the experience happens to a man who is still young enough to have the energy to rebuild anew, and the intelligence to grasp what has happened, then the experience can only produce a better and more complete person.

There was nothing unusual, therefore, in Muhammad Ali's ambition to regain the world heavyweight title. He had won it, fair and square, and defended it many times with honour and success. It had been taken from him in circumstances which were highly questionable, to say the least. Revenge is a base motive, and not one from which to launch a come-back, but the motivation, the compelling urge to regain that which one has lost, is frequently confused with vengeance. In some cases, revenge is the impetus, but it is a destructive emotion, and one which is ultimately doomed to failure. In Muhammad Ali's case, his desire to regain his title was likely based on a number of factors. The first was that he was still one of the world's greatest boxers. He had the tools. The second was that he had had a great series of good wins over most of the world's high ranking heavyweights, so he had the capability. The third reason, and this is the one which is most frequently confused with revenge, was that he needed to beat both Norton and Frazier because he had lost through his own failures, and not because he had been an inferior fighter. He had overestimated himself, and had not prepared well enough for either fight. Although it can be argued that the jaw injury sustained in the fight with Norton was an accident, Ali knew, deep down inside, that Norton would never have been allowed to land that punch if he, Ali, had not allowed him to do it. He had lost through his own failings, and not through the superiority of his opponents: therefore his own pride and integrity were at stake.

At first, he had to beat Norton, but even before that, he had to make sure that his broken jaw had healed perfectly. He had to enter this fight as fit as he could be, for time was no longer on his side.

The first round was dominated by Ali: it was clear that Ali remembered well his man from their last fight. Ali meant business, and had sized Norton up very early on in round one. Ali's speed was as fast and as dazzling as it had always been, and he picked off Norton with rangy jabs. To the absorbed onlooker, however, Ali's jabs could have been more accurate. There was something in the way Norton moved which was unorthodox, and it occasionally seemed that Ali did not always have the measure of his man. But the opening round was clearly Ali's, and any doubts were but passing clouds on the distant horizon. In the second round, which was similar to the first, Ali continued his relentless pursuit of Norton with a continuous display of fleet footwork, and dancing, jabbing blows to Norton's head. If he carried on like this, then Ali would surely win — but a complete victory meant a knockout. In the third, it appeared that Ali was aiming for just that, for he charged from his corner, unleashing a relentless succession of deadly firepower, concentrating on Norton's head, jabbing, hooking and raising the temperature of the fight by many degrees. Norton, to his eternal credit, appeared ready for this: he had studied the character of Ali's recent fights, and, knowing the best method of defence is to attack, he counter-attacked Ali with rights to the head and body. The crowd were certainly spectators to a real fight, with neither man willing to surrender anything at all. In the fourth and fifth rounds the temperature fell back somewhat, but Ali was clearly ahead on points. He had won the first three rounds, and possibly the fourth and fifth as well, but he had also seemed to have abandoned any hope of an early knockout. Norton turned the tables on Ali by adopting his habit of leaning backwards — which any boxer is told never to do, within ten seconds of getting in a ring for the first time. By leaning backwards, especially to one side away from the attacker, the danger to the defending boxer is obvious, but if it is judged correctly, at the moment the attacker had tilted his centre of gravity forwards, then the attacker misses, uses energy needlessly, and psychologically is put on the defensive. This was a new situation for Ali, who had used it himself many times on other boxers, and he did not always manage to successfully overcome Norton's tactics. The sixth round again showed a marked loss of pace from Ali, which appeared due to tiredness rather than a change of approach. From this round it was Norton who got on top, his age and sustaining power appearing more resilient than Ali's. Ali really did begin to look tired: his reflexes were still there, but their speed had slowed alarmingly. Gradually, the rounds began to go Norton's way, but it was clear that Ali's early lead was so great that nothing short of a knockout or severe damage to Ali would end the fight in Norton's favour.

By the tenth, Ali was in serious trouble: Norton's persistent attacks were paying off, not because his ability had become more finely-tuned, but because Ali had metamorphosed into a comparatively static target. His feet would not move, and Ali fans became worried at the change in their man since the sparkling start to the fight. In the eleventh, Ali slid further down: flat-footed, apparently a pathetic relic of the man he once was, Norton had little difficulty in unleshing his considerable punches into Ali's body. At one time, Ali could do nothing to prevent having to absorb five consecutive body blows: all he could do was to draw on the purely physical side of his defensive armour. He had proved before that he had the capability to absorb punishment. On this occasion, he had no choice: any pre-fight boasts were hollow echoes on the ether as Norton prepared to repeat his success of twenty-three weeks before.

During the interval before the start of the twelfth, Ali must have realised that he was close to defeat, for he came out at the start of the final round as though propelled by whirlwind energy. With both hands flying, attacking, slugging — hardly pausing for breath, Ali tore into Norton in a clear attempt to overwhelm him. At first he succeeded, as Norton was staggered by Ali's attack. Norton's knees appeared rubbery, and Ali forced him back on the ropes, the avenging warrior poised for the kill. But Norton had something left: mustering up his final reserves of strength and courage, he counter-attacked Ali, taking him to the ropes. Ali would have none of this — his left hand, with the force of a rocket, tore into Norton's face and body, fit to burst through Norton's defending arms. This was a fight, indeed: the crowd, electrified by this rousing finale, were on their feet, urging their encouragement to the protagonists in ever-growing roars of volume. Locked in the corner, slugging it out until Doomsday if need be, neither Ali nor Norton heard the final bell until Dick Young prised them apart.

It was over, and on a split decision Ali had earned his victory: as on their first meeting, it had been close. Ali had climbed, rather than leaped over his first hurdle, and Norton had been put back in his place.

Norton's two fights with Ali did everything to enhance his career. To have defeated Ali, inflicting such punishment first time around, and to have come so close to beating him a second time, showed Norton was no patsy, and had to be taken seriously.

Strangely enough, there was little comfort for Ali. He had won, but only just and on this showing it still seemed that to defeat both Frazier and Foreman would be asking too much from a man whose spirit was as strong as ever, but whose flesh had begun to show rather more of the advancing years than he would have liked. However, if a study of Ali's fights teaches us anything, it is that a fight should never be predicted on the basis of the one that immediately preceded it.

(2)
October 20th 1973
v RUDI LUBBERS (HOLLAND)
venue: Jakarta, Indonesia
Muhammad Ali: 15st 5lbs (215lbs)
Rudi Lubbers: 13st 13lbs (195lbs)
Referee: Enrique Jiminez
Attendance: 35,000

After the second Norton fight, it was disclosed that Ali had sustained a fracture to a finger of his right hand during the sixth round of that bout. This must have had some bearing on Ali's inability to put away Norton as commandingly as he would have liked, but it had healed quickly, for less than six weeks after fighting Norton he was in the ring again, in Jakarta against Rudi Lubbers, the Dutch boxer. Sixteen months previously, Lubbers had been rated 34th in the *light*-heavyweight division (one down from heavyweight). No-one — not even Lubbers— could possibly have thought in the Summer of 1972 that by October the following year he would be fighting Ali, and his chances against Ali were slim indeed. However, few predicted successfully the outcome of Norton's first fight with Ali, but that is just about all that could be said in Lubbers's favour. In many ways this fight with Lubbers was the least interesting of Ali's career, but each fight of Ali's tells us something different about him, and the match with Lubbers had two faintly curious ingredients. The first was Ali's need, after his narrow win over Norton, for a 'warm-up' fight before meeting Joe Frazier. The opponent should clearly not have been anyone who might remotely upset Ali's plans and Lubbers was the ideal boxer. The second was that, while it was obvious from a very early stage that Ali could have despatched Lubbers at will, he refused to do so, being content to string out the fight to the full twelve rounds, comfortably winning on points. This is the more puzzling reason. The nature of boxing traditionally demands that a fighter should make the most of his opportunities. If Ali's 'killer instinct' had been a little suspect on occasion since his return to professional fighting, it was completely absent against Lubbers. Joe Bugner, the British champion, had experienced some difficulty in overcoming Lubbers: as Ali rated Bugner more highly than some British commentators, the coming bout with the Dutchman did not appear quite so one-sided to Ali as it turned out to be.

From the beginning, Ali was master of the fight. He danced as before, but at half-speed, almost jogging in his easy pace. His jabs against Lubbers's head and body were planted more for accuracy than to cause damage. Lubbers, in turn, was possibly somewhat overawed by Ali, as he was not really in the same class, and this could account for his ineffective showing. All through the bout Ali kept Lubbers at bay, almost like a big cat toying with a mouse, totally in command of the situation. The crowd, unused to big-time boxing, loved it: rather more than the boxing buffs, as a new twist to professional fighting was given during the interval between rounds ten and eleven, when Ali, discarding the ministrations of his seconds, answered questions during a mini-interview with members of the press corps. This saved him a bit of time in the usual post-fight press conference, but possibly a comment or two from the boxing correspondents stung Ali, who came out for the eleventh with a good deal more determination than he had shown before. He caught Lubbers with a perfect uppercut, straight to the jaw, which shook the Dutchman. But that was all, for Ali failed to capitalise on it, and lapsed into his air of nonchalance. He had shown he could still go twelve rounds with ease. His next fight was the long-awaited return bout with Joe Frazier.

(3)
January 28th 1974
v JOE FRAZIER (USA)
venue: Madison Square Garden, New York City
Muhammad Ali: 15st 2lbs (212lbs)
Joe Frazier: 14st 13lbs (209lbs)
Referee: Tony Perez
Attendance: 20,748

Almost three years before, on March 8th 1971, Joe Frazier had become the first man to beat Muhammad Ali in his professional career, in a fight which has to be considered one of the great fights. Since that defeat, Ali had gradually come back, and had created for himself an undisputed right to a rematch with Frazier. Frazier himself had not been idle, either, but he had lost his world heavyweight crown to George Foreman. Before Ali could meet Foreman, he had to give the long-awaited return bout with Frazier.

The fight started at a cracking pace, which those who had seen Ali's second fight against Norton felt simply could not continue. Both men went after each other. Both unleashed powerful bombs, not always connecting, especially a fine right cross to the right hand side of Frazier's face from Ali which whizzed past Frazier's head. Frazier blocked many of Ali's punches and attacked in turn, going for Ali's body with Ali quick to slip into a hugging clinch to dampen Frazier's aggression.

The second round continued in the same way, with Frazier landing more punches this time. This was not because Ali had slowed up — he had not — but because Frazier was sharper. Frazier was more able to carry the fight to Ali, to pin him in corners. Ali had learned on their first meeting that he could take the best Frazier had to offer, and still come back smiling on the attack. Ali kept up his barrage for a further four rounds, and it was clear that even if he seemed to have little success in stopping Frazier's incessant advance, he was building up an almost insurmountable lead on points. As if to confirm this, Ali changed his attack in the seventh round. Instead of going for Frazier's legendary thick skull, through and around his guard, he sprang up from below, swinging as he went, but rarely successfully. This gave Frazier the chance to use clinching tactics, and there were rather more of these in this round than one would have liked to see, but on balance it was Frazier's round. Ali knew that his change of attack would take time to get through, and in the eighth Frazier, sensing that Ali might do something drastic, caught Ali again on the ropes and unleashed a fearful combination of punches to Ali's head. Ali, for the first time in the fight, appeared much slower on his feet, and was unable to dance away from Frazier's attack. He had to stand and take the punches, but this time he

96

was secure in the knowledge that Frazier was not going to put him away. As the round neared the end, Ali came forward, his speed discarded, and slugged it out with Frazier, then and there, in the centre of the ring. The relentless nature of Ali's attack took Frazier by surprise: he must have known that he had given Ali almost everything. Would he have to go 'right back home to get the punches that finally put him away' this time? Surely not, but in the opening part of the ninth round Frazier upped his action markedly. This took a lot out of him. It did little to disconcert Ali, who came back very strongly in reply to finish the ninth with a fierce flurry of deadly punches. Ali opened the tenth with a continuation of the fiery action, hurting Frazier with the sheer number and accuracy of his heavy punches, and kept up the pressure in the eleventh, too, catching with a notably powerful left hook to the face. The final round was all-action powerhouse stuff: the tremendous momentum generated by the accelerating action of the previous rounds here ran on ceaselessly, as both men endeavoured to bring off the Big Punch that would have settled the matter beyond dispute. But the strength and will of these two fighters prevented either from going down.

At the end of the fight Frazier's face was badly mis-shapen, but Ali's remained unmarked. The decision of the referee and the judges was unanimous: Ali had won, but there was a sizeable minority who thought the decision should have gone the other way. Not everyone who witnesses a fight will always agree on a particular decision, and although the decision in this instance was unanimous, Frazier had fought an exceptionally fine fight. Having beaten Ali once, he came close to doing it again, for the margin of Ali's win was not great. If a couple of rounds had gone to Frazier then the result would have been different. In retrospect, the decision could not be faulted.

And so, having beaten both Norton and Frazier (albeit by slim margins) Ali had removed two of the obstacles which stood in his way. The one which remained was George Foreman.

Who could have predicted, after Ali's sensational defeat by Ken Norton the year before, that within ten months he would have made such a staggering recovery? Now the pressure was on Foreman, and the tide was flowing for Ali.

(4)
October 30th 1974
**v GEORGE FOREMAN (USA) HEAVYWEIGHT
CHAMPION OF THE WORLD**
venue: Kinshasa, Zaire
Muhammad Ali: 15st 6½lbs (216½lbs)
George Foreman: 15st 10lbs (220lbs)
Referee: Jack Clayton
Attendance: 60,000

Ali's ability to draw the biggest crowds in boxing, even though at times
he held no title, has always meant that people such as Frazier and
Foreman, though they were world heavyweight champions, could never
ignore the threat he posed. The charismatic personality and universal
popularity of Muhammad Ali obliterated much of the recognition that
was due to other fighters, and his very presence — quite apart from his
public needling and flair for publicity — posed a constant harassment
that demanded settling, once and for all, in public.

Ali had won against Norton and Frazier, but in a manner that tended
to leave both fighters anxious for a third fight apiece, but against
Foreman he had his big chance: to become once again the undisputed
heavyweight champion of the world.

The venue, Kinshasa in Zaire (formerly the Belgian Congo), was
appropriate for a fighter who had allied himself with the aspirations of
his fellow-blacks in the United States, with their growing pride and
identity, for Zaire was one of the largest of the many African countries
which had gained independence from European Colonial rule during
the 1960s. During training, Foreman sustained an accidental cut
around his right eye, a week before the fight was acheduled to take
place. Consequently, the bout had to be postponed from September
24th to October 30th for it to heal. The delay served only to increase the
tension.

Unlike Ali's recent fights, Ali did not come out dancing and jabbing.
After a token start, he retreated to the ropes where he appeared to evade
Foreman's punches easily, beating the champion to the counter-attack.
There are athletes who seem instinctively to know what their opponent is
going to do next. This talent gives them the appearance of having all the
time in the world to move and consequently, the appearance of a grace
and lithe suppleness of movement of almost aesthetic appeal. This fight
had these qualities — but on one side only. By half-way through round
one, Ali showed an almost somnambulistic sure-footedness and
elegance which added yet another dimension to his myriad personality.
This may appear somewhat high-flown language to describe a
heavyweight boxing match, but it is an accurate representation of the
beginning of this extraordinary fight. How could George Foreman seem

so inept? What was it that made Ali so much the master of the bout, with hardly a minute gone? Both men were fine athletes, at the peak of their physical condition, fighting in a neutral country, having trained for many weeks for this highly important match, with so much at stake on either side.

Having made a mockery of Foreman's opening attack, Ali now rushed him with a flying combination of punches crashing about his face. Ali dominated round two, in much the same way as the first: Ali baited Foreman, almost deliberately putting himself in danger to draw the champion across the ring and expose his weaknesses. Ali evaded Foreman's best punches, and absorbed those which found their target. Ali's timing had to be split-second: a fraction too late and he could be caught by those flaying Foreman fists, and a fraction too early in counter-attacking and he could have been hitting air. The difference between the two men was surprising — Foreman was cumbersome, lumbering, dragging his slow length along, whereas Ali appeared mercurial, appollonian, striking his opponent almost at will — until Foreman suddenly caught him and momentarily impeded his flight. On such rare occasions we glimpsed the natural power of Foreman's muscular strength, but Ali could punch too and just before the end of the round he caught Foreman with a powerful right cross to the head. Ali's methods assumed greater clarity as his incessant blows to Foreman's head began to worry the champion. Ali knew this, too, for during this round his taunts could be heard all round the ringside, and he continued them during the interval, shouting derisively across to the glum Foreman.

Round three, and the pattern of the fight seemed to have established itself. Once again, Ali manoeuvred to the ropes, an oscillating target for Foreman's energy, and in so doing gave a physical demonstration of a scientific fact. Human energy, like almost all other forms, is finite: when it is discharged, it must be used constructively for it can never be recalled and used again. If it is not used in this way — if, as in the case of boxing, it continually misses its target — then the energy is useless, like a shell exploding aimlessly in the sky. An animal, if threatened, will sometimes lash out blindly in all directions, as if the mere use of raw energy will itself provide the means of escape. Lacking intelligence, the animal will not be able to think its way out of the problem, and if it has exhausted its physical energy (like a car whose petrol is wasted as its wheels spin aimlessly in the mud) then it becomes a spent force, at the mercy of its predators.

Foreman, of course, certainly never lacked intelligence, but he lacked subtlety and the ability to change his tactics as it became clear that his usual method of attack — a purely physical, energy-burning, non-psychological aggression — was not going to prevail. In round three, one could see that Foreman was beginning to run out of steam, and Ali, himself sensing this, struck home with an immensely powerful

99

combination again to Foreman's head and upper body. The punches clearly shook Foreman, who was so perplexed as the bell went that referee Clayton had to escort Foreman to his corner. Foreman's apparent lack of resilience was even more marked in round four: this was one of the very best rounds of boxing skill Ali can ever have fought. First, his attacks were launched from an unusual position for a fighter clearly in the lead — within a few feet of the ropes; secondly, his incessant left jabs landed with deadly accuracy at all times on Foreman's lunging, stubborn head; thirdly, Ali himself was unhit, countering and fending-off Foreman's heavier punches with icy disdain. Last, and perhaps most important, in psychological terms Ali had already won.

In round five, Foreman again made a valiant effort to floor Ali, who, as puzzling as ever, went to the ropes. This time, his attitude seemed suicidal, as he called Foreman to hit him, exposing his face and body to Foreman's fists. Foreman took full advantage of the gift. He hit Ali several times with full force. The crowd gasped at this, but Ali, his unquenchable spirit actually feeding from Foreman's attack, literally bounced back from the ropes, with fierce shouts to Foreman, urging him to do his worst. Foreman swung again and again, but it was slow-motion stuff compared to Ali. Foreman actually hit Ali comparatively frequently in round five, and for all Ali's verbal taunts, points are awarded in boxing for hitting the opponent, not for shouting at him. Foreman probably won round five, but it was largely academic, and as round six progressed it seemed the ending could not be far away.

Once more, Ali placed himself at risk on the ropes, occasionally — perhaps from boredom (!) — moving away to hit Foreman, and then moving back again to stand there, arms covering his head like a floppy teddy-bear, as Foreman's progressively weaker punches failed to find their mark. It was an extraordinary fight — surely this could not be so one-sided? — and yet it seemed as though there never was any doubt as to the winner almost from the start. In spite of the punches of Foreman, there had been so few that Ali was never in danger. The crowd, too — and remember, it was 3.00am in Zaire, 60,000 people had turned out to watch this event — sensed the one-sidedness of the bout and began to shout at Foreman, booing his apparent lack of stamina. Foreman, if he could make out the roars of disgust, could do nothing — he had not gone more than two rounds in his last eight fights. His stamina was suspect, but more importantly, he had never fought anyone like Ali before. Less than six minutes in the ring with each of one's previous eight opponents might do wonders for the ego, but it does not make one an experienced boxer. The root cause of Foreman's impending defeat was his lack of experience.

In round seven Ali moved again into the attack. His left hand homed in with devastating speed and power, before a right to Foreman's body gave the first glimpse of an impending knockout. Foreman lurched against the ropes, and almost went through them. The sequence of

100

punches from Ali was spell-binding — goodness knows what it was doing to Foreman — and the full-throated roar of the crowd called for blood. Foreman would not give in: at the start of round eight he staggered out and hit Ali three times with rights to the head. In the first few rounds these punches would have really hurt Ali, but at the moment they meant little, mere distractions in the remorseless fate of the fight as Foreman swung again, his own momentum causing him to stumble and fall. Up again he came at Ali, who met him half-way with two rights. A left and right to Foreman's exposed head and Foreman bent forward, slowly toppling to the floor like a stunt man dying in an indifferent film. Slowly, with commendable courage, Foreman rose to his feet, but Jack Clayton got to ten first. Foreman didn't live there anymore.

And so Muhammad Ali had achieved the impossible — once again, through his own merits, he was the undisputed heavyweight champion of the world, and who could cavil at his tremendous, almost unbelievable, success. This was his moment, and no-one else's — the certain master.

The nature of the win was astonishing: ten years and ten months, almost to the day, after first winning the heavyweight crown from Sonny Liston, Muhammad Ali had regained it, but with a display of skill that no boxer should, or could, emulate. He completely flummoxed Foreman by doing the very thing that all fighters are taught not to do. He waged this fight from a position of defence, almost always on the ropes, lurching backwards away from Foreman's punches, diving around to evade his swings. And yet, as the film shows, he hardly moved at all. There was little dancing, no hit-and-run: how did he do it? Ali's corner simply could not believe the way in which he won — it went against all the training he had undertaken, all the pre-match bragging about dancing for fifteen rounds. He had fooled everyone, had told them what they probably wanted to hear, and in so doing had got Foreman to come to the ring prepared to counter Ali's dancing. When the fight began, he didn't dance, but used his speed in a new way, largely from the waist up as well as absorbing the best his opponent could offer. Foreman, whose lack of experience had been largely overlooked, could do nothing to counter this absolutely perfect win. It was a demonstration of total boxing skill allied to a deeply subtle form of tactical strategy which repays the closest study.

CHAPTER ELEVEN

Champion for the Second Time

(1)
March 24th 1975
v CHUCK WEPNER (USA)
venue: Cleveland, Ohio
Muhammad Ali: 15st 13½lbs (223½lbs)
Chuck Wepner: 16st 1lb (225lbs)
Referee: Tony Perez
Attendance: 14,847

With his superlative win over George Foreman, which again made him undisputed world heavyweight champion, Muhammad Ali was again able to defend his title freely in his own country and abroad. After Foreman, Ali waited five months before his first title defence, against Chuck Wepner, in Cleveland. On paper, it looked to be a predictably easy fight for Ali: even though the champion was thirty-three, Wepner was too years older, and had never been rated high enough to pose a serious threat to the world's leading fighters. In the event, the contest again showed the danger of predicting fights — although Ali won comfortably by a knockout, and was way ahead on points, Wepner gave Ali a few frights. The first was that Wepner was only stopped in the final thirty seconds of the last round (round fifteen); the second was when Wepner floored Ali in the ninth with a piledriving right to Ali's ribcage. The third surprise was the appearance of tiredness and listlessness which infected Ali's performance.

There is no doubt that Ali's win over Foreman had thrilled him to the depths of his soul: there is almost always a reaction, a relaxation after a great triumph, and the champion's additional weight against Wepner indicates that he did not prepare himself as thoroughly for this fight as he should have done. However, in the opening rounds, it was soon apparent that Wepner was a very powerful man who, unlike Foreman, lacked nothing in stamina. He kept coming forward, with far greater variety in his attack than Foreman had shown, apparently undeterred by Ali's flashing jabs. Ali tended to coast a little in this fight early on, seeming unconcerned to put his man away, nor was Ali fighting with the same brilliant determination as he displayed against Foreman. In the early rounds, Ali showed a little of his dancing and jabbing, but he soon gave up the dancing part, and the contest, after round four, became much more serious and earnest in purpose than had earlier seemed the case. Ali may well have realised that he had underestimated Wepner, whose vast experience showed he was more than capable of weathering Ali's intermittent squalls and storms, and the fight became a match of slugging and battering after round six. In round nine came Wepner's punch which knocked Ali down. Ali sprawled on his back, but, somewhat impetuously, jumped up at three rather than taking a count of eight or nine. Back on his feet, Ali tore into the challenger, unleashing an angry burst of punches all round Wepner's head and body. On this occasion, it was Wepner who gave Ali a lesson in soaking up punishment for he refused to go down even though he was hit repeatedly.

Ali cut Wepner's left eye and then his right eye also, and blood oozed down into Wepner's eyes. It was not too serious, however, for his seconds were able to repair the damage enough for the fight to continue. From the tenth round on, Ali tried every ounce of strength to get Wepner to go down, but he still would not quit. In the thirteenth and fourteenth, Ali stepped back to lower the pace, and varied his attack, lobbing fewer punches into Wepner's face, doing great damage, scoring in the process. But Wepner, for all Ali's superiority, remained immutable. As the bell sounded for the final round, Ali rushed at Wepner with a blast of punches that forced Wepner back. These formed the *coups des grâce*, for Wepner, waving his arms in a fruitless attempt to hit Ali, blundered forwards and sideways, and fell, catching the ropes as he went. While on the floor, he still refused to be beaten, and using the ropes he managed to pull himself to his feet, ready to box on. Tony Perez, the referee, stepped between them, and, looking into Wepner's glazed unfocussing eyes, stopped the bout, at two minutes, forty-one seconds of the final round.

It was a surprising fight: tough, rugged, brutal and remorseless. There was little skill, and the few things which Ali must have learned from it were that first he should no longer underestimate his opponents, and secondly to be quite sure that he still had enough speed to move away from trouble. Although he paced himself through this fight, there is no doubt that he would have liked to finish it sooner. It showed he still had the stamina to go fifteen rounds, as he might well need to, should he rematch with Frazier, Norton, or Foreman.

(2)
May 16th 1975
v RON LYLE (USA)
venue: Las Vegas
Muhammad Ali: 16st 0½lbs (224½lbs)
Ron Lyle: 15st 9lbs (219lbs)
Referee: F. Hernandez
Attendance: 6,513

There was considerable interest in Ali's next fight, against Ron Lyle. Lyle was an experienced fighter, and ranked quite a way higher in the world heavyweight listings than Wepner. Against the background of Ali's battling win over Wepner in the final round, and the fact that this fight occurred only eight weeks after the meeting with Wepner, there were some who thought that Ali's stamina would be put in jeopardy.

The fight began in classic Ali style, with dancing and quiet appraisal of his opponent. There was little action in the opening round, and Lyle was given no chance to land his best punch, his left, but in the second and third, Ali gradually opened up the fight, scoring with sure punches and jabs to Lyle's head and body. Lyle fought well, not being intimidated by Ali's stature (in every sense) and connected several times with Ali's jaw. Lyle also showed himself a master of ringcraft, superior in this regard to either Foreman or Wepner, and he had clearly done his homework. He refused to be drawn, either onto the ropes or into clinches, and persisted in a laudable attempt to fight the bout on his own terms. It says much for Lyle's strength of character and his all-round ability that, although he never looked at any time as if he would floor Ali, he appeared a difficult man to beat. Ali had shown he could handle old-fashioned sluggers on many occasions, but against Lyle he had rather more to do in terms of style and technique. Lyle was wily, and Ali was overweight, and his dancing would also take its toll of his reserves of energy.

After the fourth, by when he had built up a good lead (the first four rounds were clearly Ali's), the champion relaxed a little, perhaps mindful of his age as he kept Lyle at bay. This brought the expected cries of hurt rage from the crowd, who had paid to see a bloodbath presumably, but it was a shrewd move on Ali's part. Ali was thirty-three, and the world champion, and it was his turn to play the waiting game, to spread his energy, forcing his partner into expensive errors which would drain his power. Ali had predicted before the fight that Lyle would go in the eighth, and in the seventh, as if to make his forecast come true, Ali attacked again, but Lyle had been in the boxing ring long enough to see that coming a mile away, and it seemed that he, too, had stored his energy until then. Lyle met the challenge in the seventh and the eighth, countering Ali's surges with penetrating left jabs which frustrated Ali's attempts to close in for the kill, and even caused the champion's nose to bleed. Ali soon realised that his ploy had been foiled, and he backed away, pacing himself for another eruption. This was not long in coming: after two rounds of less-than-dynamic action, Ali caught Lyle clean on the jaw with a good right hook. This visibly shook Lyle, and Ali, seizing his chance with the verocity of a tiger, unleashed a spontaneous flurry of combination punches that could only be appreciated fully when played back in slow motion on the video machine. Lyle needed no reminding, for he finally went under the fury of this attack, staggering against the ropes, hemmed in and finally pummelled to the canvas. Ali had done it again.

(3)
June 30th 1975
v JOE BUGNER (GREAT BRITAIN)
venue: Kuala Lumpur
Muhammad Ali: 16st 1lb (225lbs)
Joe Bugner: 16st 6lbs (230lbs)
Referee: Takeo Ugo
Attendance: 10,000

Ali's second fight with Joe Bugner was his third title defence within four months: no-one could accuse Ali of failing to defend his title regularly. It was apparent that, world champion the second time, Ali was prepared to defend his crown as frequently as he had when he was champion ten years before. To those who had seen Ali's two previous fights (against Wepner and Lyle), Ali's weight was proving something of a problem, for on more than one occasion during those fights Ali appeared a little the worse for wear. There were those too who felt that as Joe Bugner had the advantage of being ten years younger than Lyle and also possessed a decidedly more powerful left hand than Ali's last challenger, his own track record of having gone the distance against Ali two-and-a-half years before meant this bout in Kuala lumpur could be reasonably close. On these factors, and his own record, Bugner was a worthy challenger.

Once again, the pre-fight pundits were proved wrong, though for reasons which were difficult to predict at almost any time before the fight. If any one factor contributed to the sense of disappointment which hung over the fight, it was the almost insane decision to hold the match in the tropics at that time of year. As Ali and Bugner came into the ring, the temperature at the ringside was in the high eighties. The strain and drain on the physique of each of these big men was immense from before the opening bell. In the circumstances, it was clearly not going to be a match of great action and fast movement.

The temperature and humidity quickly took their toll of both fighters, for in the opening round Ali was content to circle Bugner at about a third of his usual speed, sizing him up to see if there had been any noticeable change in Bugner's methods. The only change was that Bugner had started at below his best form. Bugner appeared to stumble towards Ali, rather than move effortlessly towards him, and hardly landed a decent punch in the opening round. Both men soon fell into the habit of getting involved in clinches, which tended to drag the momentum of the already faintly soporific fight down to an even lower level. Rounds two and three were much the same, with neither boxer showing any willingness to take the fight to the other. Perhaps Ali was puzzled by Bugner's leaden approach — the British boxer was clearly having an off-night, and in the circumstances it is strange that Ali did not attempt to put Bugner away early on, and so save everyone a great deal of trouble. One reason may be that although Bugner was unaggressive and lacked vim, he was still a very big man, and tough, too, and Ali still retained a great deal of respect for him. This could, therefore, have been one of those few occasions in Ali's career when he over-rated an opponent's chances. Another, more plausible, reason was that Ali might have already had his eyes on his next fight, which was scheduled against Joe Frazier, and this was almost certain to prove a tough and lengthy fight. Maybe Ali had to prove to himself that even in stifling conditions, he had the stamina and resolve to stick it out for the full distance. He had seen what happens to a fighter who gets out of the habit of fighting over a long distance: his defeat of George Foreman proved that, and he had no intention of allowing himself to fall into the same trap.

This is, however, to paint a rosy picture of much of this fight: to the onlooker, it was a depressing experience, for if Bugner was having an off-night, then Ali seemed far below his own peak, as well. Neither man could raise the level of this meeting above the faintly mediocre — it always takes two to make a fight, and the will to win seemed strangely absent from both Ali and Bugner. In fairness, one must point to the sweltering conditions under which the match was fought: this was little consolation to those watching, but there was the odd flash of magic. In round thirteen, Bugner began to hit out and landed several quite good punches, but Ali, quickly retaliating, would have none of this. The crowd voiced their derision at this burst of life, which was akin to a tiny spontaneous combustion in a desert, but without the raw material or the breath of wind to fan the flames into a burning fire of excitement. It was all too much to expect, and was not helped by Ali appearing very tired by the effort. He overcame this tiredness in the last two rounds, and continued jabbing Bugner to the end, which was only broken by their continuous holding and clinching as they paused for breath in the fetid heat. In another atmosphere, things would have been different, but Ali coasted easily to a points win over Bugner, whose lack-lustre showing disconcerted his many supporters. After the match Ali admitted that it was probably not a good fight to watch, but few spectators, sipping their ice-cold drinks during the bout, could appreciate the oppressive atmosphere, up there in the ring, in which the fighters were expected to box.

(4)
September 20th 1975
v JOE FRAZIER (USA)
venue: Sports Arena, Quezon City, Manila
Muhammad Ali: 16st 0½lbs (224½lbs)
Joe Frazier: 15st 5½lbs (215½lbs)
Referee: Carlos Padilla
Attendance: 20,000

This fight was the first time Ali had fought anyone professionally on three occasions. For this 'Thriller in Manila' expectation ran high, for Frazier had narrowly won the first encounter, and Ali the second by an equally narrow margin. Both fights had been particularly memorable, and billed as 'fights of the century'. Ali, by staying on in Kuala Lumpur after his win over Bugner, was anxious to acclimatize himself as thoroughly as possible to tropical temperatures before moving on to Manila. He had trained very hard for this fight, and it is possible that Ali had used his two previous fights as warm-up bouts for this match. In saying this, one does not underestimate either Lyle or Bugner, but merely to point out that there were those who felt — with some justification — that Ali's three previous title defences since his defeat of George Foreman hardly showed him to be as great a champion as he had been ten years before. Fight fans knew that this was the Big One.

They were not disappointed, for, in a match which more than made up for any failings in his earlier fights, Muhammad Ali, and his opponent Joe Frazier, on their third meeting fought one of the greatest heavyweight bouts of all time. A true 'fight of the century', for once the publicist's puffs were accurate. This has to go down as possibly Ali's greatest fight, which utterly dispels any blind prejudice that kept his name from 'rolls of honour', 'halls of fame' or other 'old pals' acts' Only a truly great champion, and a truly great boxer, could have brought off this win against Frazier. Both men deserve the gratitude and praise of all boxing enthusiasts for their composure and bearing during and after this meeting.

Apart from the demands of the fight itself, Ali was beset by personal problems. His second wife, Belinda, had left the training camp suddenly, twelve hours after arriving, to go home, complaining of Ali's association with another woman. After the fight, Ali attempted to dismiss his wife's anger as being a publicity stunt, but it turned out that Mrs Ali had grounds for complaint.

Against this background of personal and professional pressures, the fight began. It started at a cracking pace: Ali came out quickly, as did Frazier. There were no preambling formalities this time, for Ali was already snaking long jabs after the weaving and crouching Frazier, and landing them, too, as though this part had been rehearsed before. In a sense it had, and what could not be denied was Ali's superiority in reach and height — he made them tell, and tell again, in the first round, catching Frazier with sudden combinations and pushing him backwards. To Frazier, at first these blows seemed like sand in the face of a seasoned nomadic traveller, as he brushed them airily to one side in his continuous attempts to get under Ali and engage him from below. Ali, however, knew what Frazier intended, and his speed, clever punching and delicate movements evaded Frazier's more impacted blows. All the while Ali was attacking, flicking Frazier, worrying that bullet like head, which refused to be swayed. Suddenly, it was the end of the round, and the high seriousness and sense of purpose with which the fight had begun made the onlookers breathe an easeful sigh of relief. It had been an absorbing first round, with no frills or furbelows, just intent and serious boxing. The high skill continued in the second, as though a brief moment had merely interrupted the continuous action, For Ali's attacking stance and sudden breaks backwards piled the pressure even more intently upon Frazier. Frazier, in turn, was not interested in Ali's speed or other antics, however seriously they might be applied, for he had ideas of his own. There was nothing that would prevent him from regaining his title, he seemed to imply, as he stalked the faster man inexorably. He caught Ali with several nasty-looking blows, but Ali in turn — his ability to absorb the worst any fighter could offer was by now well-known — was himself unlikely to be upset by the power of these intermittent blows. Gradually the arms and fists of the two combatants seemed to metamorphose into incessant rain, as though it was a stark, naked conflict of two absolutely indomitable wills, meeting on a supernatural plane, but physically in a boxing ring. The fists were just points of contact, like moves on a chessboard. It was a fight — a real one, this time — between two men, two *personae*, and neither showed any intention of being defeated by the other. Ali's speed was riveting, as was the power and fearful accuracy of those incessant jabs and combinations. Surely this was another case of the champion piling up a sizeable lead at the outset, at the same time as wearing down his opponent, in order to be in for a killer round about the tenth or eleventh. To the know-all fight fanatic, perhaps; but if anyone knew about Muhammad Ali in the ring, it was Joe Frazier, and bitter experience told him that to let Ali get away just a little would mean giving him a lead which would be almost impossible to catch. Frazier, at the start of round three, began fractionally to take the initiative, and to pummel Ali more and more insistently: Ali, in turn, adopted a slightly relaxed stance during the round, as though the effort of the first two rounds demanded a breather, but he also knew that Frazier would be a difficult man to stop. If the fight was to go the full distance — as it very well might — then Frazier should not be allowed to get ahead on points. Ali was not clowning here, not looking at the audience, nor shouting abuse at his opponent, as he had in their first fight, with tragic consequences. In this third, decisive, meeting Ali stood firm, deadly serious, his face a mask of fierce concentration. Frazier, however, could play poker too, and he kept up his intense, remorseless advance in round four. Ali was more than a match for him, and although he may momentarily have lost the initiative he had so convincingly built up in the first two rounds, he was certainly ahead by the end of the fourth session. During the interval, the tension hardly subsided as both men glowered across the ring at each other: there was no acting this time, no false arrogance. Just a determined, oblique earnestness in their fixed stares.

In the fifth, Frazier again lifted himself around the obstacles of Ali's long arms and snaked under several times. He forced Ali back on to the ropes, and Ali, unable to take advantage of them in the same remarkable manner as he had when fighting Foreman, showed his superb defensive mechanism by covering his head and fending off Frazier's vicious blows as though deflecting driftwood on a high sea. After several seconds, Ali would move away and again come on the attack, catching Frazier across the rib-cage, just under his heart, and stopping his insistent onward movement. This time, however, Frazier kept himself firmly under control and balance. In the sixth, Frazier continued with taking the fight to Ali, who, rather more on the defensive than one would otherwise have thought, had to take a lot of punishment in this round. It was clear he could take it: he appeared, after the barrage had subsided, no worse off than before, and mounted a powerful counter-attack, aiming again at Frazier's head, as if to crack through its legendary thickness and granite-like density. By the end of the sixth the fight was evenly poised. Each man was giving of his best — it was clear that by this time it had almost become the fight of both men's lives — and it had developed into a thoroughly superb and absorbing contest. In the seventh the pendulum began to swing gently towards Ali, and then with increasing certainty, more so, as he mounted a fierce attack on Frazier which at last stopped the iron man's advance. In no way was Frazier prepared to go down — if at all — but he seemed to wilt occasionally at the force and speed of Ali's brutal challenge. By the end of the seventh, Ali had wrested the initiative back again, and it needed a greater effort on Frazier's part to mount another withering counter-attack in the eighth. There was no way either man was going to be suddenly beaten, as the war of attrition was being waged on both sides, but as the bout swung first this way and then that, the sheer fascination of the immense drama being fought out half a world away appeared to obliterate all outside thoughts. Frazier's counter-attack in the eighth, like in the third, continued into the next round, and he possibly took the ninth on balance. Ali, however, secure in the knowledge that it was he who was marginally ahead on points, and not Frazier, was not disconcerted by Frazier's outburst. If anything (although hindsight is always the best viewpoint from which to describe any event) it seemed as though Ali was prepared to let Frazier win a round or two at this time. However, Ali's will to win was so enormous, so consuming in its certainty that any temporary advantage Frazier might take would doubtless not be at Ali's bidding: Frazier himself wanted desperately to win this contest, and felt no doubt that, having beaten Ali once before, he could well do it again.

Ali tore after Frazier in the tenth and eleventh rounds, this time appearing to stop rather more effectively than before Frazier's trenchant punching. Ali's blows seemed to take on superhuman form when, time and time again he landed combinations, uppercuts, and stabbing jabs to Frazier's head and body. Frazier still had it all to do, for the difference in reach was a powerful fact of life and he had to expend more energy on coming forward than if the arms of both men had been the same length. Moment by moment, the fight dodged this way and that, with first Ali seeming to take the upper hand, only to have it countermanded the next second with a particularly fine piece of boxing from Frazier. Gradually, however, the skills of both men began to pale into insignificance against the strength of their bodies, as, grappled together in a struggle which transcended time and place, they epitomised a manner of conflict which sought no victor or vanquished. In a fight of this magnitude, of this stature, structure and sheer courage, incredible pace and tremendous passion, there could, in truth, be no loser. It was a triumph for both men.

But boxing does not end like that: there had to be a winner, and Ali grasped that point just that little more fiercely and with greater dedication than Frazier. In the twelfth, Ali came out as if possessed, and launched another amazing attack on Frazier's body: where was the energy coming from? How on earth could this man sustain this immense fire-power? Was this the same man who had been reduced in stature by forces of nature when fighting Joe Bugner? Of course it was the same man, but here stretched to the very limits of his being, his complete virtuosity and inner strength being laid bare for all to see as he strove within an inch of his very life to overcome his adversary. The fourteenth round continued on this same high level, with Ali now attempting to squeeze the last ounce of effort from his straining, punished body. Frazier, amazingly, still came forward, like a Yeti through a blizzard, and one shuddered in admiration at this man's unquenchable ardour. The passion and drama of the fight was strained to fever-pitch — Ali caught Frazier with a sickening blow to the jaw which sent Frazier's gumshield flying from his mouth, still joined to it by a spurting parabola of blood. The champion closed in, hitting his man again and again with the frenzied justice of a warrior-hero, causing Frazier to stop, stumble again and wither under the almost inhuman punishment.

110

But Frazier could take it: still, in the closing minute of round fourteen, he found the strength to go after Ali, to try and catch him and to turn the tables on the champion. But as the round ended, it was Ali again who tore into his man, forcing his opponent to submit, and attempting with all the power at his command to get him to go down. How could Ron Lyle have knocked Ali down, while Frazier could not? How could Frazier have withstood this shattering, brain-jarring, nerve-screaming onslaught? As the final seconds of the round ticked away both men were in the centre of the ring, slugging it out, but it was Ali who inched himself above Frazier in consistency of attack.

During the interval, Frazier's seconds tried to repair the damage done to his face and to revive him, but the sixty seconds Frazier had to rest on the seat meant his body had begun to register the beating he had taken from Ali. He was all in: his will was finally bent: if not snapped for ever — for at this moment of truth, humanity took over from the titanic struggle we had witnessed. Frazier could absorb no more: his seconds called over the referee, Carlos Padilla, who agreed that Frazier should not come out for the final round.

And so Muhammad Ali had won the most momentous and prodigious fight he had ever fought. It was a colossal achievement, and afterwards Ali praised Frazier's fighting ability and courage: "He is great. He is one hell of a fighter. It was one hell of a fight." It was indeed.

CHAPTER TWELVE

Still Champ: On The Road Again

(1)
February 19th 1976
v JEAN-PIERRE COOPMAN (BELGIUM)
venue: Roberto Clement Stadium, San Juan, Puerto Rico
Muhammad Ali: 16st 1lb (225lbs)
Jean-Pierre Coopman: 14st 7lbs (202lbs)
Referee: Ismael Falu
Attendance: 12,000

Following the epic and heroic struggle to defeat Frazier at their third meeting, Ali's fifth title defence of his second tenure of office appeared a mere bagatelle, an incomparably easier proposition for the champion.

Coopman (always referred to by Ali as 'Cooperman') was little known, for he had only fought once outside of his native Belgium, when he was knocked out during round four of a non-title fight by Harald Skog of Oslo, in January 1973. He had also been beaten by Rudi Lubbers in ten rounds two years before, but these defeats do not tell the full story. Coopman had been dubbed the 'Lion of Flanders' owing to his very good record: out of twenty-seven bouts he had only lost three. This record also made him a strong contender for the then-vacant European Heavyweight Title, which had been vacated by Joe Bugner. In fact, Coopman's manager, Charles de Jaeger, had undertaken to match Coopman with Richard Dunn of Britain for this vacant title. However, the offer from Muhammad Ali's camp conflicted with this, and, even through the Dunn contract had already been fixed up, Coopman was withdrawn at the last minute to prepare for the Ali fight. The European Boxing Union banned Coopman for two years for this action, and withdrew de Jaeger's licence for life.

Ali had settled in to the El San Juan Hotel in the Puerto Rican capital, but the day before the fight he was hurriedly evacuated from the building as a fire broke out in the kitchens on the ninth floor, immediately above Ali's suite. Firemen fought for an hour and a half to control the blaze, which started just after midday. Those who thought these exciting events were an omen were disappointed. Twenty-four wins out of twenty-seven or not, Coopman's class of opposition within

112

Belgium was nowhere near that necessary for him to come within spitting distance of beating Ali. The Belgian stonemason from Ingelmunster started as though he intended to make a fight of it, seemingly unimpressed by Ali's stature, but soon an air of defeatism crept into his manner as Ali, moving swiftly enough around his man, started picking him off, blow by blow. This was a different world after Joe Frazier, and in the second and third rounds Ali so completely reached his total superiority over Coopman that the gallant Belgian could do nothing to break the physical and psychological grip of the champion. In the fourth, Ali broke out of his mood and crashed several speedy combinations into the Belgian's body, staggering him, and followed up with blows to the head. This was not a lengthy attack, but it was enough to signal the end of Coopman. In the fifth, winded by the buffeting he had received the previous round, Coopman appeared to be near the end of his strength as Ali cornered him for the kill, an eruptive right that caught Coopman full on the jaw and sent him to the canvas.

It was an easy win for Ali, a further demonstration and reminder — if any were needed — that, apart from one or two contenders worthy of challenging him, there was virtually no opposition at that time to this all-powerful, all-conquering athlete.

(2)
April 30th 1976
v JIMMY YOUNG (USA)
venue: Landover, Maryland
Muhammad Ali: 16st 6lbs (230lbs)
Jimmy Young: 14st 13lbs (209lbs)
Referee: Tom Kelly
Attendance: 12,472 announced*

Prior to this fight, Muhammad Ali had been invited by President Gerald Ford to attend a function at the White House. This was the first official invitation by a United States President in the whole of Ali's career, and marked the end of any lingering resentments at Ali's stand against the draft — at least, in official circles. As it was election year in the USA, cynics pointed out that Ford's gesture was probably a vote-catching one — as a Republican, he needed to take votes from the Democrats, who were more than likely able to count on a larger share of the black vote than the President's party. The function was a state dinner for King Hussein of Jordan, who was then on an official visit to the USA. It was a pleasant prelude to the fifteenth title defence of Ali's career.

---

* although this attendance figure was that announced at the fight, most commentators noted there were not many empty seats in the 19,000 capacity auditorium

Jimmy Young came from Philadelphia: at the time he met Ali he was ranked third in the world heavyweight lists, having been a welder and docker by trade. His appearance reflected his rugged occupations, and he had scored a significant win in 1975 by outpointing Ron Lyle in Honolulu.

However trim and sharp Young looked, Ali's appearance caused a few gasps: at 230 lbs he was clearly overweight, and not just from President Ford's hospitality. By the end of round two, it appeared that Ali had seriously neglected his training. He was very much out of condition, and his lack of application in preparing for this fight showed that he did not take Young's challenge seriously. He was mistaken by doing this, for, to many people's utter surprise, Young was more than a match for Ali's tactics. The contest was televised live — a very rare occurrence — and there was at first more than a suggestion that the fight was being padded out by Ali in the early rounds to ensure the correct number of commercial breaks could be made to accommodate the advertising spots. If that seems an unworthy comment, then one has to seek the most arcane explanation to discern why the opening rounds were so bereft of action from Ali. The champion demonstrated an implacable defence, unwilling to break out against Young. Young, in turn, flashed several good-looking punches at Ali, who had replaced the famous shuffle of earlier years with a newer style, shuffling rather than a shuffle, and the occasional pawing aim towards Young's head. By the end of round four of this exhibition, Ali had done hardly anything of note, and Young had no chance of getting through the impacted defence. If Ali was playing a waiting game it was a curious one, for he moved forward defensively, daring Young to hit him. Occasionally, the wary Young, uncertain as to what Ali could be up to, obliged, but his punches were so ineffective that one could hardly believe what was going on. No sooner had Young replied to Ali's jibe than Ali suddenly flicked out a stinging right, as if to chastise Young for daring to take up the challenge. Young showed that he could duck and weave out of trouble, as Ali could ten years before, and in round four, apparently angry at Young's defensive tactics, Ali began to hit out at the challenger with a number of cracking punches. Young ducked again and again and Ali's combinations waved ineffectively in the air as they missed their target. This was frustrating for Ali: he had begun badly, clearly below par, and in danger of being made to work hard to beat the agile and self-confident Young, whose personality seemed to grow greater in confidence as he realised the effectiveness of his defensive tactics. The fight took another unrealistic turn as Young landed cross counters to Ali's head, and yet another as Young did nothing to follow up the openings which presented themselves, for no sooner had he connected than he backed away allowing Ali to shuffle forward. The champion aimed punches at Young's jerky head, and Young's bobbing and weaving lacked the ease and style that characterised Ali's. Young appeared ungainly, without the sense of purpose that would have made all the difference.

And so this strangely unreal boxing match continued, with neither man appearing to have the instinct to attack and pursue his adversary, until in round ten Ali began snaking out long looping crosses to Young. In round eleven, Ali continued his attack, and landed a hefty right cross to Young's chin, which snapped his head back sharply. This was the action the crowd had waited for so long: Young recovered quickly, however, and mounted a spirited counter-attack at Ali's head. The crowd urged Young on, and he responded with further blows which connected with Ali's body. Greatly encouraged by this, Young bounded from his corner sensing for the first time that the title could possibly be his, and he unleashed the full extent of his firepower at the champion. Ali appeared angry: he counter-attacked fiercely, and both men fell into a clinch with Young causing the hiatus. This prevented Ali from striking further blows, and when they parted Young ducked again — straight through the ropes and almost out of the ring. Ali appeared ill at ease: the fight was scrappy and awkward, not proceeding along the lines he would have wished. Young still looked able to go the full distance, and persisted in his ungainly hit-and-run manner, but Ali appeared much the more tired man. Young's ducking and weaving low, again landed him in trouble: he was forced to take standing counts, which detracted from his performance and the rhythm of the fight, and at the beginning of the fifteenth we saw a tremendous effort from Ali to knock out Young. Young's reactions, to his eternal credit at this late stage of the fight, were sharp and clear: Ali missed repeatedly, and those shots which did land were not strong enough to put Young away. And so this unhappy fight lurched to its fitful conclusion.

A sizeable proportion of the crowd thought Youhg had won: indeed, if he had not played himself into trouble in the second half of the fight — and especially in the closing rounds — he might just have carried the day, but the unanimous decision of the referee and judges was that Ali had retained his title. After the fight, at the ubiquitous press conference, Ali frankly admitted his mistakes. He had underestimated Young, he said, and acknowledged that age was creeping up on him. "I always thought that I could defeat age with my ability, but I see that age does play something." Curiously enough, Ken Norton, his opponent in his next title defence, fought on the same bill, and took a menacing win over Ron Standen. One wonders what Norton thought of his chances against Ali on the champion's showing against Young. For Ali, he could take stock of himself, he was clearly overweight, and he must have realised that if he was to remain champion for very much longer he would have to lose weight and take his training much more seriously. Those fans of Ali, who had been shocked by his appearance and lethargic performance against Young, fervently hoped he would heed the advice.

(3)
May 25th 1976
v RICHARD DUNN (GREAT BRITAIN)
venue: Olympiahalle, Munich
Muhammad Ali: 15st 10lbs (220lbs)
Richard Dunn: 14st 10½lbs (206½lbs)
Referee: H. Thomser
Attendance: 7,000

Richard Dunn, at thirty-one, became the fourth British boxer to fight Ali, yet until a few years before this meeting, any suggestion that he would be fighting Ali for the heavyweight championship of the world would have been laughed out of court. Since coming under the tutelage and management of George Biddles, however, Dunn's capability had improved out of all recognition. He had lost 9 of his 32 fights, but he had won the previous 5 consecutively, and had begun to make an impressive name for himself in his own country.

On record and technique, few would have given Dunn much of a chance against Ali, but Ali's last fight against Young had been one of the least impressive of the champion's career, and Dunn possessed two priceless attributes. The first was courage — or, more properly, spirit. Dunn had endeared himself to many boxing fans by his open-hearted willingness to fight, and he was a man who stood for a great many honest and decent qualities. The second asset was his contented and enormously enthusiastic family. His wife had made it her business to provide Dunn with a secure and loving home and hardly an interview went by without the boxer paying a tribute to his adoring family.

A few days before the fight, Dunn had reached the peak of fitness, and he was at his very best when he met Ali. His main suspect feature was his so-called 'glass jaw' — which had led to him being knocked out on a couple of occasions. But against this had to be set the fact that he was a southpaw, and would therefore be only the second such fighter to oppose Ali — the first being Karl Mildenberger, ten years previously. Ali dropped by Dunn's training camp and inevitably began the verbal wind-up. Dunn is a man of few words, and his rugged appearance and big stance (at 6ft 3ins he was Ali's equal in height), caused Ali to call the Bradford scaffolder 'Frankenstein's Monster', and could not resist the 'Dunn is going to get done' homonym. Dunn, unafraid of heights of several hundred feet as a scaffolder, was unmoved by these jibes. Ali took this fight much more seriously than his last. Young had given him a fright, and he worked hard and long to prepare himself, shedding 10lbs from his flabby weight against Young.

As the bell signalled the start of the fight, Dunn came forward to meet Ali, and, fearing nought from any man, opened up with an attack to Ali's face and body. Those English fans who had travelled to Germany for the fight could not have hoped for a more determined or purposeful beginning from Dunn, and it was some time before Ali got to grips with Dunn's awkward southpaw angle of attack. Ali, circling Dunn and trying to size him up, was caught several more times in the course of the round before he retaliated, and the champion's timing appeared faulty. Dunn's opening round was the best by far of a British boxer against Ali since Henry Cooper's first meeting. As the fighters sat awaiting the bell for the start of round two, an expectant buzz ran around the stadium. In the second, Ali's speed began to tell against Dunn, and Ali danced around him to the 'other' side, and landed good accurate jabs. Dunn kept coming forward, in so doing continuing to score. It is a matter for conjecture as to the outcome of the fight had Ali met Dunn at the same weight and in the same frame of mind as he fought Young — he surely could not have used his speed then, and would more than likely have had to take many more of Dunn's massive blows. Nothing is more fruitless than to speculate on 'what might have been', but what was beyond dispute was Dunn's spirit. He certainly had the will to fight Ali, and to go after him, as he relentlessly followed him across and around the ring, stalking the champion and presenting in turn an awkward target. In round three, Ali realised that something more was needed, and he charged into top gear to attack Dunn. Almost immediately, Ali unleashed a ferocious barrage of combination punches around Dunn's head, but when he had finished, Dunn was still there, still coming forward, like the British Infantry advancing at the Somme. Dunn counter-attacked and, according to Ali, hurt the champion with his punches. Some British commentators were at pains to belittle Dunn but fighting of this courage and determination — if lacking much in comparison to Ali's natural ability — was in the true spirit of boxing, and was something that had not been seen in an Ali fight for some time. It is a great compliment to Dunn that Ali took his challenge as seriously as he did: his training with its hard attention to his roadwork meant much in this regard and speak volumes for the British fighter who forced the champion to fight. Dunn may not have had much of a chance, but Ali had to work hard both before and during the fight to beat him.

In round four Ali seized the opening to Dunn's jaw, and he caught the Yorkshireman with a fine cross, which sent him down. After a few seconds, Dunn got up, and continued to come forward at Ali. It was going to take more than one knock-down to put this man away. Ali was stung to attack again: he unleashed a volley of blows to Dunn's face, and again, wilting under the fierce firepower, Dunn went down a second time. But he was not yet beaten. He got up again, just as before and, amazingly, came forward still to attack Ali, actually scoring with some jabs. Ali's anger was roused by this, and for a third time he tore into Dunn, his timing now accurate and deadly. Dunn wilted, and fell a third time. Surely this was it? But no — with immense courage, for by now whatever chance Dunn had had surely flown through the window — Dunn arose from the floor, dusted his gloves, and still made forward motions with his feet. He was on his feet — far from finished — when the bell went.

Whatever Ali thought during the interval, he knew he had to use some very powerful punches to put Dunn away. Shortly after round five began, Ali caught Dunn's face with a fearful jab, and sadly Dunn slumped to the floor. This was it — but again, no: Dunn pulled himself up and, astonishingly, came forward to attack the man who had put him down four times. Ali stared in disbelief, and unleashed another outburst. For the fifth time, Dunn fell, and took an extended count. But he got up, to the utter amazement of all those witnessing this wholly admirable courage, and still tried to come at Ali. The referee, however, had seen enough, and counted Dunn out on his feet.

It was over — Ali had won the verdict, but Dunn had won the hearts and appreciation of all those who admire the best qualities in boxing.

(4)
September 29th 1976
v KEN NORTON (USA)
venue: Yankee Stadium, New York City
Muhammad Ali: 15st 11lbs (221lbs)
Ken Norton: 15st 7½lbs (217½lbs)
Referee: Arthur Mercante
Attendance: 40,000

Ken Norton was the second boxer to fight Muhammad Ali on three occasions. The first man to do this was Joe Frazier, and each of those encounters has to rank among the best of all Ali's fights. With Ken Norton, however, some dubious questions remain — not so much about the decisions, although they were fiercely contested — but about the manner and nature of the fights. Ali had taken Frazier seriously: he trained hard, and knew that he simply had to beat him, and on their final meeting, to beat him well. This act of will on Ali's part — matched by similar honest resistance from Frazier — sparked off some truly memorable boxing, the sort that one would gladly sit through fifty mundane fights to see. But, from the first, in Ken Norton Ali found a strange opponent. Norton was inconsistent in his attack: he could not be easily quantified, analysed, planned against and beaten. One could not do that with Norton. Their first fight, in San Diego, was astonishing: Ali, out of condition, thought he would coast to an easy victory against a no-hoper with a handful of fights under his belt. Ali was seriously injured as Norton pounced and just got the decision. It really could have gone either way — it was close, but Ali knew that he had to beat Norton next time around if his career was to continue. On their second meeting, Ali got his revenge, but again it was on a split decision. Norton's followers, naturally, thought he should have won, and therefore a third meeting — the final decider — was called for. Three years had gone by since their last fight, so this close encounter of the third kind had more than a transitory significance.

In interviews following several of his previous fights, Ali had intimated that, as a tired man, he was ready to quit the ring. That was nothing new from world champions who had reached the zenith of their career — there is always 'just that one more and then I'll retire' mentality from professional boxers that leads, inevitably, to the loser's dressing-room. The third fight with Norton could have been that turning-point.

A few seconds preliminary sparring into round one told both boxers all they wanted to know about each other. They had spent 24 rounds in the ring together, so there were no secrets this time. Ali began in commanding style, brilliant, the epitome of all that was best in his fighting career, a worthy champion, for all the world able to defend his richly-deserved title with ease. He dominated Norton, dancing, jabbing, bobbing and weaving as of old. Surely this could not be the thirty-four-year-old boxer who had seemed ten years older when fighting Young, who seemed a sharp thirty-four-year-old against Dunn, and who now appeared a carbon copy of himself of ten years before? If Muhammad Ali proved anything in the professional boxing ring, it is the apparent superiority of mind over matter. Round two continued along this broad freeway: Ali was conducting the tour, pointing out the high spots and the dangers, dictating the terms to Norton, who gradually began to think his way through the labyrinthine movement of the champion. Towards the end of round two, Norton began to move forward, taking a leaf from the Richard Dunn colouring book, for even the best tour guide in the world has to stop occasionally to deal with the awkward questions of the persistent tourist.

After Ali's superb opening rounds, the third was more evenly matched, either through Ali taking a back-pedalling breather, or from Norton's more aggressive style. Norton was by now too experienced a fighter to be dissuaded by Ali's gamesmanship: the tide slowly turned against the champion who, astonishingly, would stop in the middle of a round, turn to the crowd and wave at a friend. It takes a thick mental skin not to be put off by that kind of thing: it certainly was a preposterous move in a world title fight. Norton, as if to disabuse Ali of any ideas he might have of winning a psychological battle, managed to get in close in round four, and caught the champion with several beautifully-timed combination punches. Ali's clowning stopped a little, as he realised that Norton was not to be so easily outwitted, and he backed away from the challenger in good defensive covering style. Norton pursued Ali across the ring, forcing him to retaliate. It was Norton, after Ali's dazzling opening, who turned the meeting into a fight — which was, after all, what people had come to see.

Although this was Ali's fifth appearance in a ring within twelve months, his fights with Coopman, Young and Dunn had not seen him at his brilliant best over any real distance. Not since his epic third meeting with Frazier had Ali *fought* consistently throughout the whole of a fight: this fact was a powerful psychological weapon in Norton's favour. He pursued Ali again and again, taking the fight to the champion, but, more experienced than Dunn had been (who tried a similar style), Norton was able to force Ali into making more errors. By now, Ali's opening speed had been reduced to a fraction of its earlier velocity, and Ali had lost a lot of his thrust. Experienced Ali-watchers had seen just about everything from their man, but this appeared to be the hand of old father time on the champion's shoulder. Norton undoubtedly thought so, for, with that increasing certainty that comes to those who know they are doing something well, and can do even better, Norton slowly but surely took command of the fight. Ali was forced on the defensive, and his timing came adrift.

Round seven was a humdinger: Ali took the fight by the scruff of the neck and stopped the drift away from him. He caught Norton with punches that were combinations of speed, accuracy, ringcraft and sheer old-fashioned strength. If, at the end of round six, Norton's adrenalin was running high, by the end of round seven he sat down knowing full well that Ali was one hell of a guy to beat. There were to be no broken jaws this time — Norton would have to do it without any good fortune. But fortune favours the brave, and Norton could not allow his momentum to be stopped by Ali's outburst in the seventh. Both men had resorted to snarling abuse at each other, but this was surely an involuntary reaction to the nervous and impacted struggle being waged between them. In the eighth, Norton came back to overwhelm Ali: the ding-dong style of the match had everyone on tenterhooks. It seemed that the result that neither man wanted — a close one for the third time — was on the cards.

By the ninth round, Ali knew he was running out of rounds: if anything, Norton was ahead and, from that moment on, the crowd saw a physical act of will that was quite remarkable. Norton was still firing on all cylinders, a superb testament to his assiduous training, but it was Ali who almost literally clawed his way back into the fight, countering, blocking, moving timely and with the occasional classic glimpse of poise and decisiveness against Norton, whose big and sturdy heart had, in both senses, to take a pounding.

The tenth round veered again Norton's way, as Ali seemed to lack the last ounce of gutfulness to swing it in his favour, but in the eleventh, his batteries recharged by the interval, Ali came out with a do-or-die expression on his face that was awe-inspiring to behold. He fought Norton with the tenacity and tumultuously incessant determination of a team of crack commandos, heavily outnumbered and at bay. Ali's back was almost really up against the wall as he dragged up the reserve tank of energy to combat Norton. Norton, by now as much exhausted as any man would have been in the circumstances, faltered under Ali's incendiaries, and backed-off after a particularly ferocious succession of right crosses from Ali that would surely have floored any other fighter in the world on that night. But Norton, seemingly carrying Excelsior on this occasion, refused to go down, an act of will as rugged and as tensile as Ali's had been at the end of round six. This was a fight of resolve, doggedness, and stamina, and was fought like grim death.

Ali continued his new-found onslaught in the twelfth, and again shattered Norton's hopes of taking that round by sheer perseverance. Norton was no stranger to obstinacy, either, and he knew that Ali's strength must surely tire as the fight progressed. Norton came back in the thirteenth as if to prove that Ali was a human being after all, and marginally took the round. It was probably Norton's first successful round since the tenth, and everyone sensed that the fight hinged on the last two rounds. These final rounds were like a brilliant firework display, a *coda* of immense activity and energy, blazing like a gigantic fire. The two men took the fight to each other, steady and firm as battered rocks, buffeted first this way and that, but in the end, it was Ali who had marginally overcome the grit and heart of his opponent.

Many commentators thought Ali had lost, but many, too, thought he had done enough to keep his crown. The referee and judges gave Ali the unanimous decision, but, even so, it was marginal. Norton could not believe it: surely he had done everything he possibly could have done to win? Deep down inside he felt he had beaten Ali. It was too much for him: overcome with despair at what he thought was the injustice of the result, Norton broke down in tears. It was a sad end to a memorable fight, but no-one could blame him, least of all Ali, who knew what it had cost both men. On October 1st 1976, two days after this hard-fought and narrowly-won victory, Muhammad Ali announced his resignation from the ring, in Istanbul. Many people believed they had seen the last appearance of Muhammad Ali in professional boxing, but on December 10th he confirmed to Jose Sulaiman, President of the WBC that he intended to resume his career.

(5)
May 16th 1977
v ALFREDO EVANGELISTA (SPAIN)
venue: Landover, Maryland
Muhammad Ali: 15st 11¼lbs (221¼lbs)
Alfredo Evangelista: 14st 13½lbs (209½lbs)
Referee: H. Chinni
Attendance: 12,000

Time waits for no man, and although in previous fights Ali had shown the effects of the advancing years on his speed, this fight with Evangelista was the first real indication that age was soon to prove a hurdle which could only get higher for Ali. Not that Evangelista at any time seemed able to beat Ali — that would have been asking too much — but to those who had got into the habit of thinking that Ali would always be around, and would somehow always be able to see off the opposition, must have had a salutary jolt when they learned that Evangelista was only five years old when Ali began his professional career. The champion was giving away thirteen years — and by any boxing standards, that is a lot of years to discount.

At thirty-five, Ali was approaching the final phase of his career. His previous fights had shown that, naturally, the dazzling speed of his youth had deserted him — not entirely, for there were odd occasions when Ali sparkled as of old. As the years passed by, Ali was obliged to develop other parts of his technique to compensate for the loss of persistent pace. The miraculous thing was that he had these other attributes, but, strangely enough, they were absent from the opening rounds of this fight. It was Evangelista (a naturalised Spaniard, born in Uruguay), with nothing to lose and everything to play for, who began at speed, chasing the champion and forcing the action. Ali, who looked like a cuddly old teddy bear, with an air of indifference surrounding him, appeared almost unwilling to retaliate, as if afraid of hurting the young man. Only when the young puppy snapped once too often did the bear growl and lunge, and Ali appeared to dream-walk through the opening rounds, doing little to score. Evangelista managed to get through the wall of flesh from time to time, and appeared to hurt Ali occasionally. Ali, for his part, lapsed into the puzzling habit of leaning back on the ropes, like a lazy hooker, and motioned with his gloves for Evangelista to attack him, covering his face as he responded. Why?

By any traditional standards, this event could hardly be described as a world professional heavyweight championship title fight, because it manifestly was not a fight. Ali had shown on many occasions in the past that there are many ways of beating an opponent. He had demoralised opponents even before a bout started by his psychological horse-play, to the point that no-one could say with any degree of certainty just what he meant, and what he did not mean. Ali's 'planned confusion' was so fascinating — even though (as on this occasion) it could be exasperating — that one got the feeling that people would queue up and pay good money to watch Ali do almost anything. Ali was not only the master of his opponents, the most charismatic and superb fighter possibly of all time, but also the master of the crowd. He was a great performer, like Presley or Sinatra, able to hold the attention of a big audience almost literally in the palm of his hand: like a dancer, through movement alone, without words.

All this may be interesting enough for the student of human behaviour, but to the boxing enthusiast and specialist, this was no longer good enough. Not that it had ever been, for Ali always possessed enough of the classic boxing skills to silence those critics who claimed he lacked those skills. But in this fight it seemed as though the showmanship, the crowd-pulling magic that had always been there, since 17,000 people turned out in mid-winter in Pittsburgh in 1963 to see the young Cassius Clay whip Charlie Powell, this showmanship — by itself — had motivated the fight for so long. Those to whom Ali was an amusing character, but who did not follow boxing themselves, were probably delighted at this performance: perhaps Ali was going to win a fight without hitting his opponent, but the understandable frustration of those to whom such behaviour from the world champion demeaned the noble art grew more vocal and more urgent as the non-event in the ring was played out before their eyes.

Or was it? With a paradoxical character like Ali, who is to say how hard he was trying? Maybe he just had an off-night: he had had them before, as all human beings have. Maybe this was the right way to fight Evangelista by taking all that he could throw at him, and using up little energy in return. Could it not be that, yet again, Ali was several steps ahead of his critics?

Occasionally, as if toeing the accelerator on an idling car to test that all was well, Ali would break out of his daydream, and at such moments Evangelista showed all the confidence of youth in refusing to be over-awed by Ali.

By round ten, it seemed as though the fight could go on for another thirty or forty rounds at this pace — and then, when everyone had thought they had seen it all, Ali snapped out of his trance, and began to fight. Gradually, as if awakening from a deep hibernation, Ali opened up, ever more dangerously, cutting in to Evangelista with growing frequency so that by the end Ali seemed a veritable whirlwind of punching activity in comparison to his opening dawdlings. At that moment, the whole of the final round, the fifteenth, we saw what Ali was still capable of, and Evangelista, although it never seemed as though he would beat Ali, showed the crowd that he was much more of a fighter — and a game one, too — than Ali had let him demonstrate in the first half-hour. Evangelista refused to go down, but Ali easily took

123

the verdict on points. The wily, experienced Ali completely outplayed his younger opponent, but it was age, and age alone, that dictated the manner in which Ali would defend his title. No young boxer, full of himself and supremely confident, at the peak of his condition and straining at the leash, would fight — or could have fought — as Ali had against Evangelista. It was fascinating, but it could not last for ever, a puzzling 'resumption' of his career.

(6)
September 29th 1977
v EARNIE SHAVERS (USA)
venue: Madison Square Garden, New York City
Muhammad Ali: 16st 1lb (225lbs)
Earnie Shavers: 15st 1lb (211lbs)
Referee: John Lobancio
Attendance: 14,613

When Ali confirmed, the previous December, that he intended to resume his career (following his 'resignation' after the third Norton fight) he pointed out to the World Boxing Commission that, before a rematch with George Foreman, he wanted to meet a lesser opponent. In Alfredo Evangelista he had certainly done that but, instead of following this with a meeting with Foreman, the thirty-three-year-old Earnie Shavers was his next opponent.

Since the fight with Evangelista, Ali had married for a third time, his new wife, Veronica, in Beverly Hills on Sunday June 19th. Earnie Shavers was a vastly experienced and well-respected fighter who had no intention of being a push-over. Interest in the fight was naturally high, and the bout was televised live across the USA. The fight began in low gear, with both men circling, probing gently at first, gauging the extent of reach and reaction with the skill and expertise which young fighters invariably lack. Shavers was not slow to take advantage of the occasional Ali opening, and managed to catch the champion with a couple of hard punches, scoring well and causing Ali to back-track, change gear, and gather his forces before continuing with the ritualistic opening move. In round two, the inspection continued, with neither man willing to embark on an extended attack. Shavers dipped into his repertoire, suddenly letting fly with the occasional eruptive punch, most of which missed. Ali was totally in command of himself, and at times appeared almost to be observing the contest from a distance, at one remove. This was nothing like the moon-walk he undertook in the fight against Evangelista, the reason was Shavers' surprising speed. Shavers was a man who was supposed to be past his prime (as in some ways Ali was), yet he was moving with a quickness and a lithe agility that must have

124

had Ali wondering as to his opponent's stamina. If Ali was thinking along these lines, then he must have known that as Shavers had never fought a bout which lasted more than ten rounds, the advantage would lie with Ali: as Ali had demonstrated his ability to pace himself well, he would still be going when Shavers had run out of energy. Rounds three and four continued this evenly-spaced opening sequence, with Ali never in trouble, always a little ahead, as cool as a cucumber, but probably wondering from from time to time how Shavers was to be put away.

Round five gave the foretaste of a possible answer: Ali jumped up from his stool when the bell rang, and, with a startling change of speed and tactics, unleashed a blur of combination punches on and around the bemused head of Shavers. Ali's footwork was in disco style as he brought memories flooding back of his early capers round the ring in the 1960s. It was really incredible to watch — a dazzling display of what this truly extraordinary man could do. It did not last long, however, but it must have unnerved Shavers, whose own speed, although pretty good, was never in this class. After round five, the fight lapsed into the areas of lethargy which threatened the first four rounds. Ali stopped dancing, and once more became the toddling jogger, hobbling towards his man and then, disinterestedly, with a curious display of claudication, covering his face to prevent Shavers from getting inside him. Occasionally, from within this cocoon-like stance, the butterfly once known as Muhammad Ali would set free high-velocity combinations. As in round five, Shavers was completely confused by the lightning flashes of Ali's hands. And then, as suddenly as the commotion began, Ali would again lapse back into his languid footing, ludicrously covering himself against Shavers's non-attacks, almost as though the champion wanted nothing more to do than to curl up and go to sleep.

This ploy is all right for a few times, but it is hardly the kind of title defence the public is entitled to expect from a world champion. Ali, however, always was a law unto himself — even though by adopting this pacifist approach he fell foul of the laws of the game — and swayed backwards onto the ropes in rounds eight and nine, seemingly unwilling to engage Shavers in any kind of meaningful boxing. The crowd had had enough of this — was this the spectacle that Ali had come out of retirement for? Booing, at first quiet and intermittent, soon caught on as the crowd began to cry their disgust at this exhibition, which was not funny anymore. Ali had stung the crowd, if not Shavers, and it must have struck home to the champion that if he really was still 'The People's Champion' — as in many ways he was — then it was the people who were booing him, had had enough of his jokes and fooling around, and wanted to know if he could still box.

Round five was no fluke, for at the start of round ten, Ali again found his magic dancing slippers. This was the farthest Shavers had ever been in a fight, and Ali must have thought he could have finished the match in grandiose style. By doing this he would bring the very crowd, which only a few moments before had been cat-calling him, to its feet to applaud his victory. Round ten was brilliant for Ali: fleet of foot, mobile in the extreme, with accurate punches, deliciously-timed crosses, and well-put-together combinations, which hit Shavers with considerable cumulative force. Shavers, a tough old nut, was as startled by this change of tone as he had been before, and quickly fell behind — if not on the floor, then on points — as Ali surged ahead in a span of unstoppable power and energy: he kept us this fierce barrage in the eleventh and twelfth rounds, and must have been surprised to see Shavers still on his feet, for by then it seemed that Ali was beginning to feel the effects of his outburst. In round thirteen Shavers appeared to have weathered the storm, for it was he who came forward, landing good effective punches on the champion's head and body. Now it was Ali's turn to look groggy, and the crowd, combusted by this electrifying spark of drama, roared their approval. Shavers almost floored Ali, and in the next round Ali was indeed on the floor — but it was a genuine slip, the only time in the fight when either man went down — and Shavers kept up his pressure on Ali. In the last round the fight lived up to its billing, as the final three minutes brought a welter of ding-dong action. The fortunes of the boxers swung this way and that. At first it seemed that Shavers was on the point of knocking Ali down. Then Ali recovered, and was on the point of flooring Shavers. And so it went on, the last sixty seconds almost unbearable in their tension and fierce-paced activity. On this high note the fight ended — an extraordinary fight, utterly unique, varying from the ridiculous to the sublime. Once the excitement had subsided, it was clear that Ali had done more than enough to win. But Shavers had surprised everyone that night, and perhaps even himself, by revealing a never-suspected measure of stamina and resolve.

CHAPTER THIRTEEN

Journey's End?

(1)
February 16th 1978
v LEON SPINKS (USA)
venue: Pavilion, Hilton Hotel, Las Vegas, Nevada
Muhammad Ali: 16st 0¼lbs (224¼lbs)
Leon Spinks: 14st 1¼lbs (197¼lbs)
Referee: Dave Pearl
Attendance: 5,300

Almost five months had elapsed since Ali's win over Earnie Shavers, a fight of great contrasts and mixtures. Even to the most avid Ali fan, it was clear that the champion's recent title defences had shown him to be less than at his peak. Although the demands of time, in slowing down his action, had naturally taken their toll, Muhammad Ali still left the distinct impression that there was a faintly disinterested manner about him, as though his heart and soul were not as fully committed to the tasks in hand as they should have been, and as perhaps the public has a right to expect from a great champion.

One of the most revealing things about this fight with Leon Spinks was a television interview Ali gave with the BBC commentator, Harry Carpenter, before the fight took place. In it, Ali appeared his usual relaxed self, but he seemed quite clearly to be almost bored at the prospect. He spoke of his desire to be with his family, almost to settle down and see his children grow up, to give up the peripatetic nature of his profession. Although, in human terms, these are worthy ideals, a boxer needs rather more than a pair of carpet slippers and a baby to bounce on his knee if he is going to defend the richest prize in sport. Few people — Ali included — gave the inexperienced and unrated Spinks a chance, but if Ali kept up this philosophy, the end of his career would not be long in coming.

Of course, one never really knows in many ways just what Ali means: he is such a contradictory character that Mr Carpenter could have just caught him at a particularly happy time, when Ali was at his most domesticated, but all this was worlds away from Gorgeous George, from the sneering, bragging, dominating, lean and hungry Cassius of fifteen years before. Could it be that our champion had grown old and a little tubby, purring instead of snarling? A boxer must have a killer instinct, and who could divine that in this contented father, playing with his children, at peace with the world? This is not such a fanciful assumption, for in the last few days of his training, Muhammad Ali gave up sparring, and instead confined himself to shadow-boxing, punching the heavy bag, and rope-work. Leon Spinks, like Ali, Joe Frazier and George Foreman before him, had been an Olympic gold-medallist, the latest, winning his at Montreal in 1976. Spinks had had only seven professional bouts, and was 27lbs lighter. He was also twelve years younger than the champion, and this was to make up for all kinds of other theoretical failings.

The bout began full of action: in spite of any forebodings about Ali's training and his attitude, he moved well, certainly a vast improvement over the mediocre parts of his fight with Shavers. But Spinks, too, with his more youthful body and lighter torso, moved fast. It was curious to see the apostle of speed in heavyweights, the man who was Cassius Clay, being made to look slow at times by his young challenger. However, Ali knew what he was doing: his vast experience meant a very great deal, and his precious natural asset, his vast reach, was able to keep Spinks away, and to deflect easily the wildly flung punches from the young man. By round three it was clear that Spinks's energy was quite remarkable: he kept coming at Ali, to mix an old saying, buzzing like a bee around the champion's head, and connecting often enough to score and jab and back away when needed. Perhaps by this time, Ali felt maybe he had neglected his training rather too much for comfort, but surely he felt reassured by the thought that Spinks was bound to run out of steam long before the scheduled twelve rounds were up. Rounds four and five showed Ali still moving well — indeed, astonishingly well for a thirty-six-year-old — and easily hitting Spinks, scoring, and piling up the points. By round six, the fight was becoming absorbing: this was clearly not going to be a quick dance round the floor and a knockout from Ali, nor one of those interminable sluggeramas, nor twelve rounds without action, for the pace and eager nervous energy of Spinks was fascinating. It was fascinating not just for itself — the spectacle of movement and continuous activity — but because the onlookers kept telling themselves he simply could not keep it up, and that when he faltered, the big cat would have its dinner. One assumed that Ali felt that way too, for he occasionally backed away, not from fear or a desire to move out of trouble, but to deliberately bring Spinks on, and at him, to use up this high octane fuel that was firing the young man.

But, as the fight proceeded, Spinks seemed hardly to slow up. Perhaps in rounds eight and nine, his speed momentarily slowed, as he took a breather — could this be, this challenger, this inexperienced fighter, taking a breather against Muhammad Ali? — impossible, but it seemed so. The pressure was now on Ali, and in round eight he began to take the upper hand, his old skill and determination flowing in great surges of power. Spinks had, however, achieved an early success: he had cut Ali's mouth, and this stimulated him, and the fight developed against all the odds into a ding-dong battle, the young impetuosity of Spinks against the cool experience of Ali. A classic meeting, in many ways, the venue seemed faintly strange for this match. Spinks was always in with a chance, but energy is not enough: it seemed, by round nine, that Ali had done enough to be ahead on points, and in the last three rounds, surely Spinks's thrust would begin to spend itself. But in round ten, the young challenger came out as fast as ever: he launched at Ali, with the ferocity of a young tiger, whirling around Ali's head and body, forcing him back on the defensive time and again, as he jabbed and flung all he had at the champion. Ali could do little to withstand this: it seemed as though he was caught up in a mini-hurricane, and had to keep still, for a moment, his arms protecting his face and head, just to get his bearings. It was an extraordinary round, but more was to come. In rounds thirteen and fourteen, Ali came back at Spinks, sensing that there was a chance he could lose his crown, and hit Spinks with some pretty hefty combinations. But Spinks knew his chance, too: when a big prize is within one's grasp, then one can absorb almost any punishment, overcome almost any catastrophe, to achieve it. And Spinks fought with the dedication that threw all caution to the winds: he had nothing to lose, and the whole world to gain.

The final round: the crowd could hardly believe what they saw — Spinks's energy was simply breathtaking. He tore at Ali, he battered at him, he would have climbed all over him if given half the chance to worry, badger, intimidate, disconcert, unsettle and wrench the title from the champion's head. Ali was by no means finished, but the thing which he needed most of all, a touch of speed, a litre of stamina, was just not in his body to draw upon. Nor, if the pre-fight interview was anything to go by, was it in his mind. Ali was up against the ropes, pushed ignominiously backwards by the brash Spinks, but he was up against it in more ways than one. He had run out of rounds, run out of time, as the bell rang to call the match to its end. The tension was electric. Spinks's overwhelming energy and keenness had taken the last three rounds — by any standards — but he had not been ahead by the end of round nine. Could he have done it? Was this dazzling *coda* able to lift the title? If he were not to win, he would have given Ali his biggest fright for many a long day, and earned the right to a rematch.

The results were announced: Spinks had indeed won, on a split decision, 2—1. The bald sentence, on paper, hardly conveys the astonishing nature of the win. Leon Spinks had brought off the biggest upset in boxing history since Cassius Clay defeated Sonny Liston on February 25th 1964. The underdog had triumphed, the no-hoper had won. Muhammad Ali's second tenure of the office of World Heavyweight Champion had ended after three-and-a-half years.

After the fight, Ali was full of praise for the man who had beaten him. He admitted that he had thought Spinks would be an easy opponent, and had therefore not trained seriously enough for the fight, but honourably added: "I have no excuses. I wasn't robbed. He landed some of the best punches. I was on the defensive, he was on the offensive. I should be sad, but I'm not."

And the new Champion, with the world at his feet, found the right words: "I'm not the greatest. I'm the latest."

(2)
September 15th 1978
v LEON SPINKS (USA) THE HEAVYWEIGHT CHAMPION OF THE WORLD
venue: Superdome, New Orleans
Muhammad Ali: 15st 11lbs (221lbs)
Leon Spinks: 14st 5lbs (201lbs)
Referee: Lucien Joubert
Attendance: 70,000

A few days after his defeat by Leon Spinks, Muhammad Ali flew to Dacca, where he accepted the honorary citizenship of Bangladesh from President Rahman. While in Dacca, Ali answered questions about his defeat. Naturally, there would be a rematch, and he predicted he would beat Spinks by a knockout. However, there was a little problem that needed settling. Ken Norton, having fought Ali three times, still believed that he should have got the decision on their third meeting, and pressed Ali for a fourth fight. The WBA supported Norton's plea, but Ali had already been signed to fight Spinks before the expiry date set by the WBA to meet Norton. Whatever Ali's feelings about a fourth Norton fight, he stated he had already defeated the top contenders, meaning Earnie Shavers among others, and a fourth outing with Norton was not then called for. Spinks's totally unexpected defeat of Ali changed all that, for Ali had agreed that after fighting Spinks he would meet Norton in September 1978. The loss to Spinks meant that Ali had to fight him first (and Norton very likely saw no point in meeting Ali if he was not world champion), and in March 1978 it was announced that Spinks would first defend his title against Ken Norton in May or June 1978. However, the attraction of an Ali-Spinks rematch was not only greater but more ethical. Ali had defeated Norton twice in succession, so he had the prior claim against Spinks.

Once again, the fractious and absurd nature of the 'organisations' which 'control' world boxing came into the open. Norton, on hearing that Spinks would first meet Ali, said he would take legal action to prevent the fight taking place. The WBA sanctioned the Ali-Spinks rematch, but the WBC stated that if Spinks would not agree first to a match with Norton by March 18th, they would strip him of his title. On March 19th, the blackmail having failed, the WBC declared Ken Norton the new Heavyweight Champion of the World. This was a new twist. Surely this was the first time anyone became World Champion without actually having won it, and boxing fans all over the world were incensed by the stupid and pathetic action taken by the WBC.

The British Boxing Board of Control supported the WBC action in part, contenting themselves to strip Spinks of his title. The BBBC were against awarding it to Norton by default, claiming — at least this part was correct — that the world title should be won in the ring. But the WBA, for perhaps the first time in its dealings with Muhammad Ali, was on his side, and had the stronger hand. If the Ali-Spinks rematch took place, then the world would have a real champion, and what would the WBC do then? Continue to recognise a man who had never won the title in the ring? It was a disgraceful state of affairs and again clearly showed the need for a single international body, recognised as such, without the warring factions of partisan prejudice which had done so much to discredit professional boxing in the eyes of many people.

On April 11th 1978 Muhammad Ali signed to fight for the Heavyweight Championship of the World against Leon Spinks at the Superdome, New Orleans on September 15th. A week later, in Atlanta, Georgia, Muhammad Ali said he will retire if he beats Spinks. He did not say what he would do if he lost.

As far as Ali was concerned, the question of losing did not arise. For him, the defeat had been a salutary jolt: Spinks's win had focused his mind clearly and firmly on the one objective. No boxer had ever defeated Ali twice, so that was an important psychological point in Ali's favour. Furthermore, Ali knew that he lost because he did not prepare himself well enough. As before with Frazier, but rather less so with Norton (if one accepts that the broken jaw was a chance in a million), Ali decided that regular and rigorous training was not necessary to prepare for a young fighter who had only had seven professional bouts. He lost in Las Vegas, therefore, not because Spinks had beaten him, but solely through his own slackness. To someone of Ali's pride and self-esteem, this was an unpardonable error: deep down inside, he must have known that as it was his fault, he was the only one who could put it right, and the way to do that was to knuckle down to sustained and thorough training.

However, other, perhaps greater, things were at stake: the first and most important was the world title. Few remembered that Spinks's defeat of Ali was the first time Ali had actually lost his title in the ring. Here was a golden opportunity for Ali to regain his rightful crown. But another matter soon became apparent. Prior to Ali defeating George Foreman in Zaire, thereby regaining the world heavyweight title, only Floyd Patterson had won it twice. For Ali to defeat Spinks would mean that he would become the first man in history to win the championship three times. This was another powerful reason to avoid any superficial activity and to concentrate on the job in hand. Ali, after his outings with Norton, Evangelista and Shavers, to say nothing of his first fight with Spinks, needed no reminding that age was no longer on his side. He knew, more than anyone else, what was really at stake in this rematch. To defeat Spinks would accomplish many things, but it would enable Ali to retire — if he so chose — as champion; to go out on top, and not bring his career to a close in ignominious defeat.

Early in his career, the brash and bragging Cassius Clay had poked fun ceaselessly at world-class heavyweights who were still in the ring long past their prime. Archie Moore had been set up to be the first big-name fighter for Clay to defeat, and, although Moore doubtless went into the ring to "shut that fresh boy's mouth", Clay proved, within four rounds, that the taunt he had shouted at Moore in Los Angeles was nothing more than the blunt truth. Of course, as Clay went on to become the greatest boxer the world has ever seen, Moore's defeat does not, at this distance, seem such a humiliation. But it was. There can be few more pathetic sights than an ageing boxer, long past his prime, getting into the ring knowing full well that he is going to be beaten again, just to earn some money. Muhammad Ali had by no means reached this level, but some of his closest admirers and advisers felt that he, of all people, could be in danger of being attracted by the allure of another few million dollars, and to go on when his career ought really have come to an end. His doctor for eighteen years, Dr Pacheco, resigned after Ali refused to heed his warnings that at 36, and at that level of world-class boxing, the time for Ali to quit had, in the doctor's opinion, passed. Muhammad Ali has always been his own master: he will do what he wants to do. He has proved his friends and enemies wrong on so many occasions in the past that, while he might listen to advice, it does not mean he will take it.

However, the fight in September was to be prepared for, and the prospect was enticing.

For Spinks, however, the months prior to the fight were dogged with bad publicity. The young black fighter from the ghetto, after only eight professional fights, suddenly found himself rich and famous. He was unprepared for fame and fortune. Between March and September 1978, the World Heavyweight Champion was arrested six times. He was variously charged with possession of drugs — cocaine — and driving the wrong way up a one-way street, among others. Brushes with the law are not new in heavyweight boxing history. Sonny Liston, for example, had spent five years in prison, but that did not prevent him from becoming a commanding world champion. In addition, Spinks's marriage was reportedly in a bad way and the champion's riotous life-style was not what one would expect from a top athlete. Furthermore, two of his brothers had also been arrested on various occasions during this time on more serious charges. His brother Kenneth, seven years younger, was convicted of intent to kill one Billy Dunlap, having shot him three times in the head, neck and hand in November 1977. Curiously enough, he was due to be sentenced on the morning of the rematch. Spinks's other brother, Michael, who won the Olympic middle-weight gold medal in the Montreal Games in 1976 (Leon having won the light-heavyweight gold medal at the same Games), was arrested for possess-ing marijuana, resisting arrest, and assaulting a policeman. His case was due to be heard on September 26th.

All these events, however, have nothing directly to do with boxing, but in psychological terms they put enormous pressure on Spinks. If he could overcome these problems, then the world would see what he was made of. The boxing associations had their own troubles: the WBC, having declared Ken Norton as their version of the world heavyweight champion, sanctioned a fight some time afterwards between Norton and Larry Holmes, a promising young boxer. To most people's astonish-ment, Holmes beat Norton, and so Holmes became the WBC world champion. All other organisations announced that the winner of the Ali-Spinks rematch would be the undisputed heavyweight champion of the world.

The venue, the gigantic Superdome in New Orleans, capable of holding around 80,000 people, was a suitable place for what many had come to regard as Ali's last fight. An estimated 70,000 people were inside (13,000 of them possessors of 'ringside' seats), and at the weigh-in the day before there were so many pressmen and photographers that the start was delayed for a long time, as there was no room for either fighter, and both Ali and Spinks had to fight their way through to the dais. Ali had lost only a few pounds, at 221lbs, but he appeared to be in far finer shape than the previous February: it was clear that much of his flab had been turned to muscle. Spinks had put on a few pounds, scaling 201lbs. Once in the ring, for the bout, Joe Frazier come on to lead the crowd in singing 'The Star-Spangled Banner'. He looked like a successful businessman, not a funky, raw, rhythm-and-blues shouter of his earlier days. It seemed incredible to realise that Muhammad Ali — who had first fought Frazier over seven years before — was still in the ring, still fighting, and had been world heavyweight champion over six years *before* he first fought Frazier. Could he still do it? — or were we to witness an appalling eclipse?

Leon Spinks sought outside help: he fell to his knees in his corner, and prayed for a long time. The referee, Lucien Joubert, unwilling to interrupt Spinks's supplications, shuffled his feet awkwardly, but at last, Spinks's prayers finished and, the seconds having left the ring, the fight was on. All eyes were on Ali, as he danced gently out from his corner. Immediately, he encircled Spinks, moving to his left, arms occasionally lightly at his side, flicking out a curious left jab, just to gauge the distance accurately, to make sure his memory of Spinks's measurements was true. After a minute of this foreplay they engaged, with Spinks attempting to come at Ali, to stop his incessant dancing, but the moment Spinks seemed able to land the odd punch, Ali was in there pulling his man on to him to throw him off balance, stopping Spinks from hitting him. This was a new Ali for Spinks, and even in this opening round, the truth of the situation was revealed: in almost 60 fights over 18 years, Muhammad Ali had fought just about every top heavyweight in the world — and had beaten them all. Leon Spinks was a raw, inexperienced, hopelessly outclassed boxer by comparison. What Ali was doing to him was kid's stuff — the kind of thing he himself learned all those years before from fighters such as Doug Jones. Already, in round one, it was becoming clear that Spinks's lack of experience meant he could do nothing to counteract Ali's immeasurably superior ringcraft.

This was a good start for Ali, but Ali's admirers knew that in his recent fights — in fact, since fighting Richard Dunn — Ali's stamina was certainly suspect. It was all very well to begin a fight with the intention of defusing an opponent (or "de-fanging the vampire" as Ali said, referring to Spinks's missing front teeth), but when the opponent had shown he had amazing stamina, then an early knockout was really called for. In round two, a similar approach was varied by a still-dancing Ali, who came out a trifle slower than before: after one minute, Ali did a quick 'double-take', as if to seek a way through Spinks's defence (which was good — but it meant that as early as round two he had the young champion on the defensive) even though few punches had landed from either man. Spinks began to duck and bob under Ali's loping, outstretched arms. Some of these ducking tactics were very low, but Mr Joubert did not bother to warn Spinks. Just before this, both men had become entangled on the ropes but, even on the break, there was something almost gentlemanly about their behaviour that was faintly puzzling. There seemed to be a total lack of animosity. At the bell, Spinks ambled back to his corner, probably thinking he had plenty of time left. In round three, he attacked, pushing Ali back onto the ropes: soon, however, Ali had forced the clinch, and Spinks was smothered. On the break, with Ali still dancing as of old, his timing accurate and almost always true, we could have been watching a fight from a dozen years before. Ali was mesmerising, but Spinks suddenly caught him with a couple of good crosses which blew away the reverie. Ali snapped back, and hit Spinks with several big punches, putting him firmly in his place. In the fourth, and especially the fifth, with Ali already way ahead on rounds (as opposed to points — the New Orleans rules were as basic as the blues), Spinks's inexperience was now clear for all to see. He charged at Ali, but Ali caught him with a superb cross in mid-flight with thirty seconds to go: it seemed possible that Ali might put in a knockout flurry here, but it was Spinks's turn to hold on to the challenger. Even after the bell sounded, they were still holding.

In the sixth and seventh (apart from a strong altercation between

Angelo Dundee and Mr Joubert between rounds) the fight proceeded along its almost pre-ordained way. The most fascinating and amazing thing was not the boxing itself — for there were comparatively few blows, and most of them were of little power — but Ali's continued fleetness of foot. Not for many years had fight fans seen Ali move with such athleticism and grace. He was unstoppable: an object-lesson to Spinks in what the control of mind, body and pace was all about. Ali must have known deep down inside that the title was his. After the bell, we saw something else which had been absent from Ali's repertoire for some time: the old 'Ali shuffle'. The great showman, with three steps of his feet, caused the crowd to erupt in his favour: they were now all on his side, and Spinks surely began to wonder what on earth he could do. He began the eighth as if to stop the rot, attacking Ali on the ropes. They had travelled that route before, and the holding, at Ali's behest, put a stop to it. Ali now attacked seriously, as he brought the champion to the centre of the ring, and seemed to seek the big punch. It was not there — and had not been for twenty-eight months, since knocking out Richard Dunn — but Spinks was unable to respond to the challenge. At the end of the round Ali strode to his corner, his arms raised in triumph. He knew he had won.

The next few rounds were similar: Ali maintained his dancing and jabbing, scoring, scoring all the time, using the shuffle to prepare himself, Spinks and the crowd for another close encounter. Very surprisingly, few combinations were thrown by either man, a tribute to Ali's speed, but by the tenth, Spinks had reached his lowest ebb. He appeared disinterested, dispirited, and talked to Ali a lot during the round. A big flurry of punches from Ali in the closing seconds sent the champion away with his tail between his legs. In the eleventh, Spinks attempted to pull himself up: he attacked at the start, and took every chance to hit Ali, in spite of Ali's tendency to smother the champion. On one occasion, with Spinks coming forward, Ali hit him very hard to the head, but Spinks ignored the blow, as if to show that he had some fight in him, and let fly a tremendous flurry of punches to Ali at the end of the round. Momentarily, it seemed as though one's earlier instincts could be wrong: was Spinks to do now another grandstand finish, firing on all cylinders as he had at Las Vegas? Perhaps, and it would have raised the fight to a very high level; but in the scoring system, only a knockout from Spinks would retain his crown, and such an eventuality seemed light-years away.

However, Spinks attacked again at the start of the twelfth, and Ali's dancing was enough to see the champion off. Again, Spinks marshalled his strength, and engaged Ali late in the round — they were still fighting, at close quarters, long after the bell had rung. Ali shuffled at the start of the thirteenth, still dancing, and surely Ali's most implacable opponent must have smiled in admiration at this incredible man's ability. His energy, control and stamina would have been remarkable in a man fifteen years his junior, but after the somewhat indifferent performances from Ali in recent years, it was incredible. It was now a formality: Ali came out dancing in the fourteenth, and after a half-hearted attack by Spinks at the start of the final round, Ali was still dancing, up on his toes: Spinks, realising that the fight was long over, still attempted a somewhat mundane attack in the last minute, but it was meaningless. Nothing could stop Muhammad Ali regaining his crown, this majestic progress into the history books. At no time did Ali appear to be in trouble, he was so totally in command of everything that Spinks, very early on, appeared overawed by the occasion. The result was that Ali had won an overwhelming victory in terms of scoring, but it appeared that Ali had taken the crown like candy from a baby. What had happened to Spinks? The loser was honest enough to admit that "my heart wasn't in the fight. My body was ready, but my mind wasn't. Maybe it's because a lot of things have happened since I was champion." But who could blame Spinks, when he left the reporters with this comment: "He's still my idol. I said it before the fight and I still mean it." That was the nub of the situation. He knew he could not beat a determined, superbly trained, Muhammad Ali. His heart was simply not in the fight.

And Ali? "Thank God it's over. I don't think I'll ever fight again, but I don't want to announce my retirement right away." He commented that he did not want to go out a loser.

Events had enabled him to win everything: his self-respect, the title, the third-time winner, without injury. If *he* wanted to, he could retire as champion, still undefeated, the most complete and masterly boxer of all time: without question, the greatest.

CHAPTER FOURTEEN

The Legacy

When a man has achieved much, and the time has come to study that which he has done, those who sift through the legacy of his achievement are often bewildered by the range and unpredictability of his labours. What at first might seem to be similar things often turn out to be, on closer acquaintance, vastly different. A book which chronicles the fights of a great boxer should so depict those fights that their individual characteristics are revealed. It is one thing to describe an event, quite another to understand it.

What is it, then, that has made Muhammad Ali such a great boxer? What precisely did he do that was so great? What can younger boxers learn from him? And what can we, who do not box, learn from this man's life in the ring that will enrich our own? If a study of this remarkable athlete's fights teaches us anything, it is that these fights are, in many ways, totally unpredictable. Each is unique: it is very difficult to couple Ali's fights together and show a group of them to be 'typical'. The fascination for a boxing observer is that no fight is 'typical' in any respect. There are great fights, of course, and great wins — and great defeats, for Ali has taught boxers how to take defeat stoically, philosophically, without the broken-hearted sentimentality of hammy fighters (and their hangers-on). One cannot take a Shakespeare play as 'typical' Shakespeare — how can one equate *A Midsummer Night's Dream* with *Hamlet*, or *The Taming of the Shrew* with *King Lear*? — nor a Beethoven symphony as 'typical' of Beethoven's symphonic writing — they are all utterly different masterpieces. In the same way, one cannot take any fight of Ali and say: "This is typical of Ali". The fight against Mathis — however much it may have upset the professional writers and those who came eagerly anticipating a bloodbath — deserves as much of our attention as the fights against Cleveland Williams or Joe Frazier: each has to be taken on its merits and Ali's methods of solving each problem are as varied and subtle as the problems themselves.

In heavyweight boxing, Muhammad Ali has been a revolutionary figure. In saying this, I do not refer to his religious or political beliefs: they are largely irrelevant to his boxing prowess. The revolutionary nature of his boxing should be clear for all to see. Single-handed (or rather, two-handedly!) he has wrought such a change in world boxing that nothing will ever be the same again. Quite apart from his realisation of the commercial attraction of charismatic figures, his intelligent use of media publicity, his use of non-traditional venues for heavyweight championship bouts — quite apart from all this, Muhammad Ali has revolutionised the heavyweight boxer's ringcraft. His speed, his dazzling footwork — these had never been seen before in a heavyweight ring. How could it be that a man weighing 15st or more (over 210lbs) was able to move with the lithe agility of a ballet dancer, completely bemusing the old-fashioned style of boxer, making others appear leaden-footed and Neanderthal-like against him? By training, mental attitude and ability, certainly, but by refusing to be the servant of any man — his own master, supremely confident in his high ability. The most remarkable example of Ali's influence on the younger generation of boxers is the way in which he himself has been defeated. It has been said that Ali, the arch-stylist, went the way of all flesh when he was defeated by Frazier, the great slugger. But that is only half the story, for Frazier knew well that before he could pin one on Ali, he had to catch him, and the only way Ali could be caught, in whatever round, was by matching his speed. In other words, Ali forced his opponents to meet him on his own terms, and the only boxers who have defeated him are those who grasped this essential truth.

Ali's defence, too, is often under-rated. Photos of him today show an unmarked face: no other boxer, a professional for almost 20 years with around 60 fights under his belt, can boast a similar record. He may not be the prettiest, but he is certainly the most unmarked. His defence constituted several conflicting parts. The first was, again, especially in the early years, his speed — his ability to dance away from trouble. The second was an amazing capacity for absorbing punishment, of gradually wearing his opponent out by taking the most fearsome blows that can be landed. Frazier's comment that he went "all the way back home to get those bombs that finally got him" bears this out, but a study of his other fights shows the punishment he took from other men, Bonavena for example, who really hurt Ali. No boxer likes to feel that the most powerful punches he can land apparently have no effect on his opponent: it is demoralising, sickening. The psychological effect is devastating, but only a very fit man can play this dangerous game. Ali could do this to perfection. His reflexes were amazingly good. His arms — of tremendous length, a 78½ins span — were massive oars deflecting punches like driftwood from the surge of the contest — an instinctive reaction, maybe, but coupled with the footwork, which even into his middle-thirties was still very fast for a heavyweight, and only seemed slow by comparison with his earlier years, made him formidable in defence.

Ali's speed of attack is sometimes overlooked. The second fight with Liston will always cause controversy, for there are those who maintain that Liston took a dive, scared of the threats to Ali's life from crackpot quarters. This takes some believing: if Liston was really such a coward — he had already served a five-year prison sentence — then how come he got into the ring in the first place? Surely it would have made more sense for him to have called the whole thing off, or changed the venue? Such a claim is manifestly absurd. Ali says, in his autobiography, that his punch lifted Liston from the floor, and *Time* magazine published a picture which confirms Ali's claim. Certainly, Ali hit Liston several times, and in the chapter on the fight, I suggested the earlier punch was the one which did the damage, and the second punch pushed Liston's mental control over the edge of awareness. But the speed of attack of Ali — that is the thing which so disconcerted his early onlookers, and even as late as the first fight with Jerry Quarry (his come-back fight), his speed had lost nothing of its sharpness. It just did not seem possible.

The one drawback to Ali's speed of attack, especially prevalent in the early fights when he defended his first heavyweight championship crown, was that the power of his punches appeared suspect. In other words, it seemed that the speed prevented him from marshalling his fullest force behind each important blow. There would appear to be some truth in this, for on those occasions where the pulse of the fight had slowed a little, and an opening appeared for Ali, his blows landed with much greater force than previously. There is other evidence to support this: after Ali's return to the ring in 1970, his speed did slow-up, particularly during the Bonavena and Frazier fights. Whether this was because of advancing years or lack of regular professional fights, or even through a different tactical approach, is uncertain, but what is beyond dispute is that, after his return to the ring, Ali's punches appeared much stronger and much more powerful in essence than they had done so before he was banned. It may be that this relaxation of tempo gave him the chance to increase the punches to a greater degree of power than before. Whatever the reason, there are many fighters who will verify to the power of Ali's punches, both before his exile as well as after it.

To these remarkable physical characteristics must be added Ali's powerful mental attributes. The first is his supreme self-confidence, the sort that manifested itself early on in an impatient, impetuous bragging. No sportsman — apart from Gorgeous George — went around before shouting out "I'm the greatest", "I'm the prettiest", or any other similar things: it just was not done. If Ali had lacked the ability, his mouth would have been shut many years ago, and he would have faded into the dim and distant memories of boxing fanatics. Ali's self-projection in this regard was two-fold. The first is the natural publicity which would accrue to the forthcoming fight. The second is that Ali genuinely believed his prophesies. After all, many of them came true, and of which previous fighter can it be said that many of his predictions as to the round in which the fight would end proved to be correct? Ali so psyched himself up, so puffed his own mental attitude that defeat never for one moment entered his head as a possibility. Whatever it did to his opponents, it did Ali a very great deal of good.

The other, and more interesting, mental attribute of Ali was his superfine control of pace. Because of his complete physical ability, and his positive mental attitude, he was hardly ever in any real danger in any fight. The disadvantage of adopting such a view of oneself means that Ali on occasion tended to over-rate himself or under-rate his opponents, as he clearly did with Bonavena and Spinks. But such occasions were rare, and, in almost all instances, Ali learned the lesson well. No: what stems from Ali's totally positive attitude (the teachings of Emil Coué carried to their logical conclusion) is his mental ability to control the fight. Many people have seen fighters of the past come out for each round in precisely the same way, as though they had no thought of changing the pace, of varying the attack, but simply to fight the same fight for a further three minutes. Ali became the arch-planner, the most calculating of fighters by changing — when *he* wanted to — the speed of the bout. There are three main reasons for this. The first is that it frequently totally disconcerts the opponent. During round intervals Ali's opponents would have received advice from their seconds, which would naturally be based on what had happened before. This advice would be set at nought if Ali came out at half-speed, or double-speed, or no speed at all, just standing there daring the opponent to hit him. This kaleidoscopic method of varying the tempo completely bemused many of his early opponents. The second is that a change of movement, more frequently a transitional pause in the bout, afforded Ali with a chance to retain his energy, in a sense to recharge his batteries. It is perfectly possible for any activity concerned with motion to be varied in this regard: to ease off the pressure, to take a breather, at the same time as not letting the matter get out of hand. Ali was able to do this to an almost uncanny degree. Those observers who from time to time complain of the comparative lack of action in a round (or a whole series of rounds) and then term the fight 'dull', fail to appreciate what is happening to the fight. Occasionally, of course, Ali was not always able to dictate the terms to quite this degree. There are examples of physical tiredness seeming to overtake the natural will of the fighter. In a curious way this is just another example of the same thing, but this time dictated by the body's physical requirements. If the body is tired, it needs a rest, and the intelligent fighter will attempt to alter his method of attack so that he can come back with greater effectiveness later on in the bout when his tiredness has gone. there are, of course, degrees of tiredness, and not all fighters can do this, but the main point remains: Ali was capable of completely altering the transitional movement of a fight in this mercurial manner, in order to take full advantage of the momentary relaxation it afforded him.

The third main reason for varying the pace is the variety it affords of attack, coupled with the element of surprise. If the tempo of the fight has already changed, then Ali's opponent would have been disconcerted at the disruption of the natural gait and rhythm of the fight: mentally, he would now be on edge, more nervous, less calm and collected. Ali himself, if taking advantage of the second reason, would now himself be more relaxed, able to pick his moment for renewed attack. And the third main reason now becomes apparent: psychologically, the control of the fight has already passed, without a blow having been struck to cause it, to Ali. By changing the pace, by keeping his opponent on edge, by gathering his strength for the final exertion — all these things combined to place the destiny of the fight within the total physical and mental control of Ali. There was no way he could lose — all other things being equal — as long as this superb tactical ploy remained so finely-tuned that it could be brought into use at anytime and, more importantly, remain undetected. The first four fights Ali had after his return to the ring in 1970 showed that, in one way or another, his opponents had attempted to learn something of his methods. The fast starts of Quarry, Bonavena, Frazier and Ellis all show a desire not to be overwhelmed by Ali's fighting machine, to take the fight *to* him. It is a measure of the universal professional respect felt for Ali that his opponents had to adopt this attitude. First, they had to overwhelm *him*, and then they could dictate terms. They were all unable, for one reason or another, to be the master from the outset.

Ali's preparations for a fight went far beyond most boxer's usual training. The physical preparation aside, Ali would obtain copies of films of his opponent's fights, and study them over and over again. He would get a photo or picture of the man and look at it for hours, perusing the face, trying to fathom the personality of the man he was to fight. As he said, in a brief insight into his methods in his autobiography:

"... I always take the measure of a man's movements, reach, speed, even before taking advantage of whatever openings I see. The only one-round knockout* in my record is with Sonny Liston and I attribute it to the fact that I had already calculated and timed his motions in an earlier fight . . ."

But this works both ways. The growth of twentieth-century technology has meant that we have a great advantage over previous generations. This is that a man's achievements, which are physical in part and take place in a time-spectrum, can be captured on tape or film for all time. Toscanini's conducting, Caruso's singing, Olivier's acting — all these are preserved, along with thousands of other priceless examples of our inheritance. The same is true of Ali's fights — on film, not always of the very best quality, but they are there. We can only guess at how good earlier fighters were, from early cinematography, stills or the reminiscences of their contemporaries. But with the great champions who had the good fortune to be at their peak when the

---

* he clearly means against a *rated* opponent: he knocked out Jim Robinson in round one in his fourth professional fight

141

facilities were there to preserve their endeavours, we can view again and again their greatest achievements.

Why should we do this — what, in fact, can they teach us? The answer is manifold: the skill of a boxer — or a ballet-dancer come to that — is not something to be acquired by study in the abstract. A boxer, and a ballet-dancer, both have to spend many hours of practice and exert rigid self-discipline to tune their bodies to respond to any demands that may be made upon them. Their natural ability has to be matched with experience, in the ring or on the stage, for the experience also adds its measure of teaching. There are, however, problems for the athlete which can only be solved through experience. As for any athlete, time is clearly of the essence: having reached his peak, the most he can hope for is to prolong it as long as possible. The earlier that peak can be reached, the greater the measure of experience, and the greater the chance of sustaining that high level. Anything which can be done to help the athlete solve his problems quickly is of great advantage. Young athletes today have a golden opportunity to study the great masters of their craft in detail: a film of a great footballer can be broken down to show the correct positioning, the angle of the kick, the centre of gravity of the body, the amount of swing and variance — all the things, apart from a basic skill and instinct, which go to make up a great footballer. The technological gifts enable singers to study at will the breath-control, phrasing, tone-colour, and musical expressiveness of the great singers of the past, which means that, for the price of a long-playing record, anyone can partake of the master-class contained on it.

The same is true of Ali's fights. A young boxer, wanting to know how Ali did it, can see for himself: the film can be slowed down, stopped, studied frame by frame as though Ali was alongside the youth demonstrating his skill then and there. But this is no substitute for experience: it is a great and priceless help, but as we learned in Chapter Three, by the time Ali had gained his ring experience, he was unwilling to do things in the 'usual' way. His own individuality asserted itself. First he had to learn what the rules were, before he could break them.

Those who are fascinated by boxing know that a boxing match takes on a life of its own, outside those actually participating in it. It is constantly in a state of flux, totally unpredictable in the detail of its duration, growing, developing, with high points, tragedies, dramas — a mirror of human activity and endeavour set before our eyes. Those to whom boxing is an inhuman slugging match, with unintelligent people set after each other like animals fighting in archaic cock-pits, fail utterly to see the skill, the subtlety, the combination of brain and physique, the Humanity of the Fight. The profound paradox of the fight is its essential quality: the combination of physical sensibility — acute, conscious, reactionary, keen and vivid — with physical insensibility — thick-skinned, blunt, which can frequently coalesce into pain and spasms of shock. This brings about the essence of boxing: the spectacle of man's basic animal instincts curbed and directed by his evolved creative intelligence.

The best fights of Muhammad Ali, the most memorable of his encounters, are above the surface drama of the contest, the victor and the vanquished, the physical struggle, the blood, the sweat and tears. What they teach us, apart from the literal boxing lessons, and what remains their eternal fascination, is the consistent and varied manner of an individual overcoming a succession of utterly different antagonists. Muhammad Ali's outward-looking optimism, his supreme self-confidence, his mental tenacity and sensitivity, his pursuit of excellence in his chosen profession, all these shine out from the spirit of a man who has overcome every obstacle. There are those who cannot resist any opportunity to expose Muhammad Ali's lack of formal education, as though by being unable to attack him for what he is, he has to be criticised for being something he has never pretended to be. Such odious activity is beneath contempt, and those 'critics' of Ali forget that his inherent dignity has been recognised and encouraged by some of the greatest men of the twentieth-century. This is not to grant Ali a fashionable intellectual appeal, to make him a chic figure, for he has not always been able to escape the attentions of the less-attractive of his entourage, but to show that overriding Ali's revolutionary boxing skills has been a totally positive attitude, fresh and flexible, which transcends the boxing ring. As Bertrand Russell wrote to Ali: "you are the symbol they are unable to destroy". This symbol, this man, apart from his tremendous achievement in the boxing ring, outside of it preaches peace and non-violence. By this example, he has raised the stature of his profession, himself and his fellow-men.

APPENDIX A

Calendar of Muhammad Ali's Life

1942 January 17	Cassius Marcellus Clay II born. Eldest child of Cassius Marcellus Clay Sr and Odessa Grady Clay, Louisville General Hospital, 6.35pm
1944	Brother Rudolph Arnet born
1954 September	Meets Joe Martin at Columbia Gymnasium, South 4th Street, Louisville
	Enrols as Martin's boxing pupil
November 12	First amateur bout v Ronnie O'Keefe. Won over three rounds on split decision. Weight 89lbs
1956	Wins first novice Golden Gloves title
1957	Physical examination reveals heart murmur. Withdraws from first national Golden Gloves championship
1958	Wins Louisville Golden Gloves. Defeated in quarter-finals of Tournament of Champions in Chicago. Meets Angelo Dundee for the first time
1959	Wins National Golden Gloves light-heavyweight championship. Wins National Amateur Athletic Union light-heavyweight championship in Toledo
May	Loses in finals of Pan-American Games to Amos Johnson — his last amateur defeat, and first defeat after 36 consecutive wins
1960 February	Wins sixth Kentucky Golden Gloves title
March	Wins Tournament of Champions in Chicago. First heavyweight fight
	Wins National Golden Gloves finals, Madison Square Garden v Gary Jawish

April 18	Registered with US Services for draft
April	Successfully defended National AAU title
	Participates in Eastern Regional Olympic trials, winning all three fights by TKOs
May	Wins Olympic elimination fights in San Francisco, becoming official Olympic light-heavyweight representative of US Boxing Team
June	Graduates Central High School, Louisville, 367 out of 391
July	Wins Olympic Gold Medal
	Has won all but a few (six or seven) of his well-over one hundred amateur bouts
October 26	Signs with Louisville Sporting Group for six years
October 29	First professional fight: beats Tunney Hunsaker, Louisville, on points
December	Angelo Dundee becomes trainer
December 27	Beats Herb Siler
1961 *January 17*	(Nineteenth birthday) — Beats Tony Esperti
February 7	Beats Jim Robinson
February	Visits Muslim temple for the first time.
February 21	Beats Donnie Fleeman
March	Spars with Ingemar Johansson
April 19	Beats LaMar Clark
June 26	Beats Duke Sabedong
July 22	Beats Alonzo Johnson
October 7	Beats Alex Miteff
November 29	Beats Willie Besmanoff
1962 *February 10*	Beats Sonny Banks
February 28	Beats Don Warner
March 9	Classified 1-A by US Army, pending tests
April 23	Beats George Logan
May 19	Beats Billy Daniels
May	Rated eighth in World Heavyweight League
May	Meets Malcolm X in Detroit
July 20	Beats Alejandro Lavorante
October 9	Fight with Archie Moore postponed owing to poor gate receipts
November 15	Beats Archie Moore
1963 *January 24*	Beats Charlie Powell
March	Meets Drew 'Bundini' Brown (associate trainer)
March 13	Beats Doug Jones
June 18	Beats Henry Cooper, first fight outside USA as professional

	August	Photographed at Malcolm X rally in Harlem
	November 5	Signs contract to fight Sonny Liston
1964	*January*	'Inconclusive' tests (16%) at Army Induction Center, Florida
	February 25	Beats Sonny Liston — becomes Heavyweight Champion of the World
		Fined $2,500 for behaviour at weigh-in. Announces he is a Muslim
	March	Classified 1—Y at Army Induction Center, Louisville — not qualified for induction. Adopts the name of Muhammad Ali
	March	WBA attempts to strip Clay of title
	May	First tour of Africa and Middle East
	August 14	Marries Sonji Roy, Chicago model
	September	Signs contract to rematch with Liston in November
	November 13	Emergency operation for hernia, City Hospital, Boston, four days before Liston fight
1965	*February 21*	Malcolm X murdered
	March 25th	Beats Sonny Liston
	November 22	Beats Floyd Patterson
1966	*January 7*	Marriage dissolved
	February 17	Reclassified 1—A — now eligible for induction
	March	Signs contract to meet Ernie Terrell WBA's 'world heavyweight champion' in Toronto. Terrell backs out
	March 29	Beats George Chuvalo
	March	Appeals against reclassification
	May 21	Beats Henry Cooper
	August 6	Beats Brian London
		Herbert Muhammad becomes manager. WBA recognise Ali as champion
	September 10	Beats Karl Mildenberger
	November 14	Beats Cleveland Williams
1967	*February 6*	Beats Ernie Terrell
	March 22	Beats Zora Folley
	April 1	Ordered to report for induction, Houston
	April 5	Signs contract for rematch with Floyd Patterson
	April 25	Appeals against induction on three counts
	April 26	Refuses induction. Same day, NYBC and WBA strip Ali of world title
	May 2	Mrs Florence Beaumont, supporter of Ali's stand against the draft, burns herself to

	death on the steps of the federal building in La Puente, California
June 26	Found guilty of unlawfully refusing induction. Fined $10,000 and five years jail. Ali appeals against sentence. Passport withdrawn
August 19	Marries Belinda Boyd, waitress
1968	Begins appearances as campus lecturer, TV 'personality' etc
June 18	Birth of daughter, Maryum
December	Jailed for ten days (serves eight) for 1967 traffic offence
1969 *August*	Films 'computer' fight with Rocky Marciano
November	Opens on Broadway in Musical, *Big Time, Buck White*. Show folds after three weeks
1970 *February 16*	Joe Frazier becomes world heavyweight champion, defeating Jimmy Ellis
June 15	Supreme Court rules that conscientious objectors can be motivated by religious beliefs
August 11	House of Sports announces Ali-Frazier fight for October 26, Atlanta, Georgia. Frazier, not consulted, withdraws. Ali rematched with Jerry Quarry
August 21	Birth of twin daughters, Jamillah and Rasheda
October 26	Beats Jerry Quarry
December 7	Beats Oscar Bonavena
1971 *March 8*	Loses to Joe Frazier — first professional defeat (first defeat since May 1959)
July 26	Beats Jimmy Ellis
November 17	Beats Buster Mathis
December 26	Beats Jurgen Blin
1972 *March 2*	Warrant for arrest issued for unpaid alimony, in Chicago
	Alimony paid, $44,000 deposited
April 1	Beats Mac Foster
May 1	Beats George Chuvalo
May 14	Birth of son, Muhammad, Jr
June 27	Beats Jerry Quarry
July 19	Beats Al 'Blue' Lewis
August	Buys 'Fighter's Heaven' — mountain top in Pennsylvania and builds country retreat
September 20	Beats Floyd Patterson
November 21	Beats Bob Foster

1973	*January 22*	George Foreman beats Joe Frazier in Kingston, Jamaica, becomes new heavyweight champion of the world
	February 14	Beats Joe Bugner
	March 31	Loses to Ken Norton, jaw broken in fight. Second professional defeat
	September 10	Beats Ken Norton
	October 20	Beats Rudi Lubbers
1974	*January 28*	Beats Joe Frazier
	September	Ali arrives in Zaire to fight Foreman
	September 17	Foreman injured in training: fight postponed until October 30
	October 30	Beats George Foreman, becomes Heavyweight Champion of the World for the second time. Completes autobiography with Richard Durham, appears 1975
1975	*March 24*	Beats Chuck Wepner
	May 16	Beats Ron Lyle
	June 30	Beats Joe Bugner
	September	Wife Belinda returns to USA after arriving in Manila for forthcoming fight, complaining of Ali's association with another woman
	September 30	Beats Joe Frazier
1976	*February 19*	Beats Jean-Pierre Coopman
	April 30	Beats Jimmy Young
	May 25	Beats Richard Dunn
		Makes feature film *The Greatest*, treatment of his life-story
	September 29	Beats Ken Norton
	October 1	Announces retirement in Istanbul
	December 10	Announces he intends to resume his career
		Marriage to Belinda dissolved
1977	*May 16*	Beats Alfredo Evangelista
	June 19	Marries Veronica, his third wife
	September 8	Ordered to return to serious training
	September 21	Knocked down twice and injured sparring with Jimmy Ellis. No recollection of event
	September 29	Beats Earnie Shavers
1978	*February 16*	Loses to Leon Spinks. Third professional defeat
	February 19	Becomes honorary citizen of Bangladesh, prophesies knockout in Spinks rematch
		Makes feature film *Bangladesh I love you*
	March	Ali-Spinks rematch signed before Spinks-Norton

WBC declares Ken Norton 'world heavy-weight champion'

WBA declares Spinks world heavyweight champion

BBBC refuses to recognise Spinks as champion

April 11   Spinks signs to defend his title against Muhammad Ali in the Superdome, New Orleans, on September 15

April 18   Ali says he will retire if he beats Spinks

September 15   Beats Leon Spinks. Becomes first man in history to win world heavyweight championship three times. Announces he will decide his future in six to eight months' time.

Professional Fight Record

1. Independent

Date		Opponent	Nationality	Location	Result	Ali's Purse $
1960	October 29th	Tunney Hunsaker	USA	Louisville	W 6	2,000

2. Louisville Sponsoring Group

Date		Opponent	Nationality	Location	Result	Ali's Purse $
1960	December 27th	Herb Siler	USA	Miami Beach	KO 4	200
1961	January 17th	Tony Esperti	USA	Miami Beach	KO 3	545
	February 7th	Jim Robinson	USA	Miami Beach	KO 1	645
	February 21st	Donnie Fleeman	USA	Miami Beach	KO 7	913
	April 19th	LaMar Clark	USA	Louisville	KO 2	2,548
	June 26th	Kolo 'Duke' Sabedong	USA	Las Vegas	W 10	1,500
	July 22nd	Alonzo Johnson	USA	Louisville	W 10	6,636
	October 7th	Alex Miteff	Argentina	Louisville	KO 6	5,644
	November 29th	Willie Besmanoff	West Germany	Louisville	KO 7	2,048
1962	February 10th	Sonny Banks	USA	New York	KO 4	5,014
	February 28th	Don Warner	USA	Miami Beach	KO 4	1,675
	April 23rd	George Logan	USA	Los Angeles	KO 4	9,206

Date		Opponent	Nationality	Location	Result	Ali's Purse $
	May 19th	Billy Daniels	USA	New York	KO 7	6,000
	July 20th	Alejandro Lavorante	Argentina	Los Angeles	KO 5	15,149
	November 15th	Archie Moore	USA	Los Angeles	KO 4	45,300
1963	January 24th	Charlie Powell	USA	Pittsburgh	KO 3	14,331
	March 13th	Doug Jones	USA	New York	W 10	57,668
	June 18th	Henry Cooper (1)	Great Britain	London	KO 5	56,098
1964	February 25th	Sonny Liston (1)	USA	Miami Beach	KO 7	464,595
1965	May 25th	Sonny Liston (2)	USA	Lewiston, Maine	KO 1	361,819
	November 22nd	Floyd Patterson (1)	USA	Las Vegas	KO 12	300,078
1966	March 29th	George Chuvalo (1)	Canada	Toronto	W 15	66,332
	May 21st	Henry Cooper (2)	Great Britain	London	KO 6	448,186
	August 6th	Brian London	Great Britain	London	KO 3	290,411
	September 10th	Karl Mildenberger	West Germany	Frankfurt	KO 12	211,576

3. Herbert Muhammad

1966	November 14th	Cleveland Williams	USA	Houston	KO 3	405,000
1967	February 6th	Ernie Terrell	USA	Houston	W 15	585,000
	March 22nd	Zora Folley	USA	New York	KO 7	275,000

4. In Exile from April 1967 to September 1970

5. Herbert Muhammad

1970	October 26th	Jerry Quarry (1)	USA	Atlanta	KO 3	580,000
	December 7th	Oscar Bonavena	Argentina	New York	KO 15	925,000
1971	March 8th	Joe Frazier (1)	USA	New York	L 15	2,500,000
	July 26th	Jimmy Ellis	USA	Houston	KO 12	450,000

Date	Opponent	Nationality	Location	Result	Ali's Purse $
November 17th	Buster Mathis	USA	Houston	W 12	300,000
1972 December 26th	Jürgen Blin	West Germany	Zurich	KO 7	250,000
April 1st	Mac Foster	USA	Tokyo	W 15	200,000
May 1st	George Chuvalo	Canada	Vancouver	W 12	200,000
June 27th	Jerry Quarry (2)	USA	Las Vegas	KO 7	500,000
July 19th	Al 'Blue' Lewis	USA	Dublin	KO 11	200,000
September 20th	Floyd Patterson (2)	USA	New York	KO 7	250,000
November 21st	Bob Foster	USA	Lake Tahoe	KO 8	260,000
1973 February 14th	Joe Bugner (1)	Great Britain	Las Vegas	W 12	285,000
March 31st	Ken Norton (1)	USA	San Diego	L 12	210,000
September 10th	Ken Norton (2)	USA	Los Angeles	W 12	535,000
October 20th	Rudi Lubbers	Holland	Jakarta	W 12	200,000
1974 January 28th	Joe Frazier (2)	USA	New York	W 12	1,715,000
October 30th	George Foreman	USA	Kinshasa	KO 8	5,450,000
1975 March 24th	Chuck Wepner	USA	Cleveland	KO 15	1,500,000
May 16th	Ron Lyle	USA	Las Vegas	KO 11	1,000,000
June 30th	Joe Bugner (2)	Great Britain	Kuala Lumpur	W 15	2,100,000
September 30th	Joe Frazier (3)	USA	Manila	KO 14	6,000,000
1976 February 19th	Jean-Pierre Coopman	Belgium	San Juan	KO 5	1,100,000
April 30th	Jimmy Young	USA	Landover	W 15	1,300,000
May 25th	Richard Dunn	Great Britain	Munich	KO 5	1,650,000
September 30th	Ken Norton (3)	USA	New York	W 15	6,000,000
1977 May 16th	Alfredo Evangelista	Spain	Landover	W 15	2,500,000
September 29th	Earnie Shavers	USA	New York	W 15	3,000,000
1978 February 16th	Leon Spinks (1)	USA	Las Vegas	L 15	3,000,000
September 15th	Leon Spinks (2)	USA	New Orleans	W 15	3,250,000

Index